The Children's Books of

RANDALL JARRELL

The Children's Books of
RANDALL JARRELL

by
Jerome Griswold

Introduction by
Mary Jarrell

Illustrations by
Maurice Sendak & Garth Williams

The University of Georgia Press
Athens and London

Designed by Kathi L. Dailey
Set in Mergenthaler Fairfield and Deepdene display
The paper in this book meets the guidelines for
permanence and durability of the Committee on
Production Guidelines for Book Longevity of the
Council on Library Resources.

Printed in the United States of America

92 91 90 89 88   5 4 3 2 1

Library of Congress Cataloging in Publication Data

Griswold, Jerome.
The children's books of Randall Jarrell.

Bibliography: p.
Includes index.
1. Jarrell, Randall, 1914–1965—Criticism and
interpretation. 2. Children's literature, American—
History and criticism. I. Title.
PS3519.A86Z66   1988   811'.52   87-19168
ISBN 0-8203-0991-5 (alk. paper)

British Library Cataloging in Publication Data available.

The frontispiece of Randall Jarrell is from the Library
of Congress.

for my families

Children Selecting Books in a Library

With beasts and gods, above, the wall is bright.
The child's head, bent to the book-colored shelves,
Is slow and sidelong and food-gathering,
Moving in blind grace . . . Yet from the mural, Care,
The grey-eyed one, fishing the morning mist,
Seizes the baby hero by the hair

And whispers, in the tongue of gods and children,
Words of doom as ecumenical as dawn
But blanched, like dawn, with dew. The children's cries
Are to men the cries of crickets, dense with warmth
—But dip a finger into Fafnir, taste it,
And all their words are plain as chance and pain.

Their tales are full of sorcerers and ogres
Because their lives are: the capricious infinite
That, like parents, no one has yet escaped
Except by luck or magic; and since strength
And wit are useless, be kind or stupid, wait
Some power's gratitude, the tide of things.

Read meanwhile . . . hunt among the shelves, as dogs do, grasses,
And find one cure for Everychild's diseases
Beginning: *Once upon a time there was*
A wolf that fed, a mouse that warned, a bear that rode
A boy. Us men, alas! wolves, mice, bears bore.
And yet wolves, mice, bears, children, gods and men

In slow perambulation up and down the shelves
Of the universe are seeking . . . who knows except themselves?
What some escape to, some escape: if we find Swann's
Way better than our own, and trudge on the back

Of the north wind to—to—somewhere east
Of the sun, west of the moon, it is because we live

By trading another's sorrow for our own; another's
Impossibilities, still unbelieved in, for our own . . .
"I am myself still"? For a little while, forget:
The world's selves cure that short disease, myself,
And we see bending to us, dewy-eyed, the great
CHANGE, dear to all things not to themselves endeared.

—Randall Jarrell, 1942

Contents

Preface   xi

Introduction   1

Chapter One. The Gingerbread Rabbit   23

Chapter Two. The Bat-Poet   52

Chapter Three. Fly by Night   75

Chapter Four. The Animal Family   96

Notes   133

Selected Bibliography   137

Index   143

Preface

R andall Jarrell was concerned with issues of literary status
because he was concerned that deserving authors—deserving of more readers and critical attention—might be overlooked. Many of his essays made the case for such authors, and they provided for timely rediscoveries. Leslie Fiedler points out how hard it is to imagine nowadays that Walt Whitman and Robert Frost were at one time invisible poets, "condescended to or excluded by the reigning criticism," until Jarrell, almost single-handedly, asked us to re-examine their cases.[1] If Christina Stead's *The Man Who Loved Children* is read these days, it is largely because Jarrell brought it to our attention in his essay about "An Unread Book."[2] And now that the work of Rudyard Kipling is once again being approved by the arbiters of taste, it should be remembered that Jarrell knew he was deserving all along.[3]

Jarrell's work for children is worth considering in this regard. The standard entry for Jarrell in literary reference books—"Although [he] wrote a very witty novel and a good deal of lively criticism as well, his most enduring interest as a writer lies in his poems"—makes no mention at all of his books for children.[4] Nonetheless, many children and adults have always held them in high regard.

This study intends to introduce Jarrell's children's books to new readers and add to the appreciation of those readers already familiar with *The Gingerbread Rabbit* (1964), *The Bat-Poet* (1964), *The Animal Family* (1965), and the posthumously published *Fly by Night* (1976). At the same time, it is an examination of the felicitous collaboration of text and pictures that resulted when the books were illustrated by Garth Williams and Maurice Sendak. It seems to me that Jarrell's children's books can be seen as the final fruition of his life and of his career as a notable twentieth-century American writer.

Randall Jarrell was born on May 6, 1914, in Nashville, Tennessee. Shortly thereafter, his parents moved to Long Beach, California, where they settled. When he was eleven, his parents separated and his mother and younger brother returned to her family in Nashville. Randall remained a year in Hollywood with his father's parents and grandmother.

Jarrell had fond memories of the year he spent with them (1925–1926), and his recollections of this time provided him with many autobiographical subjects for his last book of poems (*The Lost World*). When told he had to return to his mother in Nashville, Randall begged to remain and was heartbroken when his pleas could not be answered.

Back in Nashville, he lived with his mother's family, the Campbells. He was expected to be the "Little Man" and eventually go into the family candy business to support his mother. He held a series of what he called "awful jobs"—hawking papers, Christmas seals, and ribbons door-to-door. Recognizing that Jarrell was temperamentally unsuited for the candy business, his uncle sent him to Vanderbilt University.

Jarrell studied psychology, finally taking his B.S. in the

field in 1935, but he also made close friends with members of the English Department at Vanderbilt. He came under the influence of John Crowe Ransom through whom he would come to meet other notable Southern poets—Robert Penn Warren, Allen Tate, and Donald Davidson. Changing fields from his undergraduate major, Jarrell took an M.A. in English at Vanderbilt in 1939. When Ransom left for a position at Kenyon College, Jarrell and his friend Peter Taylor followed and worked there as English instructors. At Kenyon Jarrell would meet and form a lifelong friendship with another poet, Robert Lowell.

After taking a teaching position at the University of Texas in Austin, Jarrell met Mackie Langham and they married in June of 1940. Shortly after Pearl Harbor, he enlisted in the Army Air Corps and eventually served as a "Celestial Navigator" at an airfield in Arizona. His first book of poems (*Blood for a Stranger*) was published in 1942 and his second (*Little Friend, Little Friend*) in 1945.

After the war and with a Guggenheim Fellowship, Jarrell served as poetry editor of *The Nation*—a position in which he developed his highly praised critical skills in essays and reviews that were later to be collected in a volume of criticism, *Poetry and the Age* (1953). At the same time, he began teaching at Sarah Lawrence College and gathering many of the anecdotes which would later appear in his comic novel about academic life, *Pictures from an Institution* (1954).

In 1947 Jarrell accepted a position at the Women's College of North Carolina in Greensboro where, except for academic leaves, he was to teach for the rest of his life. A year later he published another volume of poetry, *Losses,* and spent the summer in Salzburg. The romantic ambience of that town renewed Jarrell's interest in German fairy tales and these appeared more frequently in the poems of *The Seven-League Crutches* (1951) and subsequent books.

Jarrell separated from his wife in 1951 and, after a divorce a year later, married Mary von Schrader. Following the publication of his *Selected Poems* (1955), Jarrell served from 1956 to 1958 as Poetry Consultant to the Library of Congress. During these years he and his wife often visited the capital's zoo and Jarrell became unusually fond of animals; they would appear more frequently in the poems of *The Woman at the Washington Zoo* (1960) and in the books that would follow.

Except for a collection of essays published in 1962, *A Sad Heart at the Supermarket*, Jarrell's interests in the 1960s began to turn more and more towards children. Robert Watson, a friend in Greensboro during these years, was to say: "He identified with children and the cozy world of the child. When we asked callers what they would have to drink, he was the only guest who would call for 'milk and cookies.'"⁵ Critics took notice of this new interest with the appearance in 1965 of *The Lost World,* an autobiographical book of poems that recounted Jarrell's own childhood. Karl Shapiro referred to the book's author as "the poet of the *Kinder* and the earliest games of the mind and heart."⁶ James Dickey said, "The poems are one long look . . . into a child's face."⁷ After Jarrell's death, Lowell noted that the theme of childhood "was for [Jarrell] what it was for his two favorite poets, Rilke and Wordsworth, a governing and transcendent vision."⁸ And Ransom, speaking of Jarrell's use of his childhood memories, was to observe: "he never relinquished [these], apparently, and at last they became so important to him that they gave a new direction to his life."⁹

This new direction included the role of Randall Jarrell as writer for children. *The Gingerbread Rabbit* was the first children's book; it was followed by *The Bat-Poet*. Home from a third visit to Europe in 1963, Jarrell roamed the fields near his house in North Carolina and brought back to his wife daily reports of "the ponies he saw, a little boy named David, and a red dog" all of which he was to include in a book called *Fly by Night.* [10] Later that year, ripe with memories of his own childhood, a story suddenly took possession of him and nearly wrote itself—Jarrell's childhood classic *The Animal Family.*

In 1965 Jarrell was hospitalized, but by late spring his health was thought to be mending and he was released. By fall he was back teaching in Greensboro. On the night of October 14, in Chapel Hill, he was struck and killed by an automobile. Since his death and under the supervision of his wife Mary, a number of translations as well as books have appeared, including *The Complete Poems* (1969), *The Third Book of Criticism* (1970), *Fly by Night* (1976), *Kipling, Auden and Co.* (1980), and *Randall Jarrell's Letters* (1985).

When someone asks me how I came to be interested in Randall Jarrell or in children's literature itself, I remember an incident in San Francisco a few years ago. I was with Jonathan Cott when he was asked, "How did you become interested in children's books?" His reply has since appeared in print, but it went something like this: he was a graduate student in England and suffered a kind of specialized nervous breakdown (was unable to read and wandered around simply staring at things); his friends grew worried and finally brought him a children's book, George MacDonald's *The Golden Key;* he read it, and it made him well. [11]

I was stunned by Cott's answer because it was my story all over again. A few years before, I was a graduate student in Connecticut studying for my Ph.D. exams and reading twelve and fourteen hours a day when I developed an *extreme* aversion to words and couldn't stand to have them anywhere around me (even going so far as to insist that breakfast cereals be kept in glass jars so I wouldn't have to face those loud and wordy boxes in the morning!). After several months, the longing to read (which had otherwise always been a part of my life) returned, but I knew that my next book (my first book after my Fall from alphabetical grace) had to be something special. I searched and searched until I discovered something just right, a children's book: Randall Jarrell's *The Animal Family*. It made me well, and the love of reading returned.

With this study, then, this former Humpty Dumpty aims to repay his debt to Randall Jarrell.

I would also like to thank "all the king's men" for helping me put together the pieces of this book so that I could repay that debt: Mary Jarrell, for her unstinting generosity and warm Introduction; Garth Williams, for his cooperation and reminiscences; Maurice Sendak, for his goodwill and the time he has taken over the years to talk with me about his work with Jarrell (many of those conversations reappear in this book); Hamida Bosmajian (*il migglior fabbro*), for first introducing me to Jarrell's work and for recommending improvements to this work; Joseph Cary, Joan Hall, and especially Francelia Butler, for their encouragement and direction when I was in need of it; Peter Neumeyer, Helen Neumeyer, and Harold Darling, for their suggestions that I embark on this project; Linda Rodriguez and Lois Kuznets, for their careful reading of and suggestions about the manuscript; and Elizabeth Makowski, Loris Green, and Debbie Winter, for their editorial enthusiasm and support.

The author would like to thank the following for permission to use excerpts and illustrations from Randall Jarrell's works.

"Children Selecting Books in a Library." Text © 1967 by Mary Jarrell. Illustration © 1967 by Maurice Sendak. All rights reserved. Used with permission. Reproduction courtesy of the Rosenbach Museum and Library, Philadelphia.

The Children's Books of
RANDALL JARRELL

INTRODUCTION

Mary Jarrell

Randall Jarrell spent most of his grown-up life writing for grown-ups. At forty-eight, three years before his death, he had written a novel (*Pictures from an Institution*), two critical books (*Poetry and the Age* and *A Sad Heart at the Supermarket*), a translation of Chekhov's *The Three Sisters*, half the translation of Goethe's *Faust: Part I*, and six books of poetry. Out in the world, Jarrell was mainly known as the author of the most anthologized poem of World War II ("The Death of the Ball Turret Gunner") and known in Greensboro, North Carolina, as the bearded professor who played tennis in the city tournaments and drove a Mercedes convertible.

All this came to a halt in February of 1962 when Jarrell was hospitalized for hepatitis and confined to bed too weak to read his mail. A letter from a Michael di Capua written on Macmillan stationary was among the get-well cards I showed him, and it was the turning point in Jarrell's recovery—and a final turning point in his literary career.

As I read that letter aloud, Jarrell's eyes lighted up for the first time in weeks. To his joy, this di Capua knew Jarrell's poetry and spotted his affinities with Goethe, Rilke, and the

1

Grimms. Di Capua asked him to choose and translate five Grimm's tales for an unusual series of children's classics. This series was the first brain-child of di Capua—a young, newly hired member of Macmillan's children's literature department. He was matching such writers as Jean Stafford with *The Arabian Nights,* Isak Dinesen with "Thumbelina," and John Updike with Oscar Wilde. Jarrell sat up in his bed and said, "Write him back for me, will you, pretty secretary? Tell him I'm sick now, but I'll start on them as soon as I can. In fact, how about stopping by the library and bringing me a collected Grimm's? In German, *naturlich.*" Jarrell smiled as he leaned back into his pillows, "What's this guy's name?" he asked. "Michael di Capua," I said and we both shrugged.

"Well," Jarrell added, "He's a mighty cultivated reader." For years he had been hoping for an editor who was well-read, who knew his work and who would have plans—enthusiastic plans—for it, an editor who would answer his letters by return mail and *not* be a writer himself. In the months ahead Jarrell found that di Capua was this person.

Jarrell's first contribution to the Macmillan series was titled *The Golden Bird* and consisted of five Grimm's stories and a short introduction for "Snow-White and the Seven Dwarfs," "Hansel and Gretel," "The Golden Bird," "Snow-White and Rose-Red," and "The Fisherman and His Wife." A second commission followed and was titled *The Rabbit Catcher,* for which Jarrell chose three stories by Ludwig Bechstein: "The Rabbit Catcher," "The Brave Flute Player," and "The Man and Wife in the Vinegar Jug."

Each completed translation brought an immediate long-distance call from a gentle voice in New York full of appreciation and interested questions—and with all the time in the world, it seemed, to listen. Soon, gift books began to arrive on Gogol, Hardy, Richard Strauss, and whatever else the attentive di Capua noticed Jarrell was interested in. Letters came every week, written in a clear and readable longhand and reporting progress on the books, plans for an enlarged edition of Jarrell's Grimm's translations, and with entertaining bits of news along the Rialto. Later on, there were requests from di Capua for a week-end date when we would come to New York and the promise he would get us—God knows how—opera tickets. When we first met our telephone friend in his cubby-hole at Macmillan's, he was shorter and much younger than we expected and *seemed* less commanding than Jarrell's other editors. Little did we know that behind those inexpensive spectacles and under that thin-ning head of hair was a Madison Avenue *wunderkind* who would be, at thirty-five, a Senior Children's Editor revered and feared the length and breadth of the trade. On our flight home, Jarrell and I marvelled at di Capua's attention span when Jarrell talked, the way he treated Jarrell as an end in himself (a person, as well as a writer with possibilities), and at the feeling he gave us of being on our side. We both laughed in mild astonishment recalling di Capua's mini-tantrum with the *maitre d'* and his tough treatment of taxi-drivers and beggars. We liked him. Many opera weekends later, on a brisk, sunny day in New York we were walking—three friends abreast—down Fifth Avenue to di Capua's newest restaurant discovery. Jarrell was saying ruefully what a long time it had been since he had written any poems and at that di Capua made his move. "What about writ-ing for children, Randall?" he asked so smoothly. "Have you ever thought of that?" And Jarrell, the children's writer, was invented.

I

Back in Greensboro, after his classes were over for the day, Jarrell and I took ourselves to the children's section of the downtown library. In the little chairs at the low tables, with a stack of books before us, we began leafing through them "to get the feel of the genre," as Jarrell quipped.

"So, that spring I often lay in our hammock outdoors," Jarrell told Aaron Kramer in a radio interview in New York, "and wrote everyday on a little story about a rabbit, and I'd read what I wrote to my wife who was gardening there. I enjoyed it. It wasn't a 'real' book, . . . But it was fun."

Although this was not poetry, it was fun in that it was something of his own in place of endlessly translating *Faust*. It did not feel like a "real" book because in his innocence of the genre Jarrell had underrated it and cooked up *The Gingerbread Rabbit* the way a master chef cooks up something playful for his child on a day off. Those familiar with Jarrell's writing for grown-ups will notice how he stuffed and spiced *The Gingerbread Rabbit* with familiar and not-so-bland Jarrell ingredients but sugared them over for the palate of a child of five.

Gone with the wind is Jarrell's old nemesis, the black-breasted witch-mother (of his poems "The House in the Wood" and "A Quilt Pattern") who fattens her boy to roast in the oven. In *The Gingerbread Rabbit* the witch-mother is replaced by an angel-food-cake-mother who bakes savory surprises for Little Mary after school.

Likewise the rabbits in these pages are cozy and adorable— as nowhere else in Jarrell—and treated as fluffy comfort-symbols, similar to his own pet rabbit given him by his grandparents the year he stayed with them in Hollywood. Nowhere in this book is the usual caged, helpless, victim-symbol rabbit that hops feebly in "Stalag Luft," "A Bird of Night," and "A Street Off Sunset"; nor, as in "A Child of Courts," the rabbit that dies "for a use"—like Jarrell's own childhood rabbit did after the boy returned to his mother in Nashville and his down-to-earth grandparents made a meal of the pet.

Introduction

At first the babyish, guileless, doughy gingerbread rabbit seems destined for the same cruel fate but, after giving him a fright or two, the author sets him on the road marked Happy Ending. There, the orphan-hero is saved from the jaws of a fox by a fatherly, "big, brown rabbit" who with "Darling" his wife wants to adopt him and have him sleep in "a little rush bed" and feed on "tiny, golden carrots." In the end, their offer brings tears to the gingerbread rabbit's little raisin eyes, and he exclaims (as Jarrell did, vainly, to his grandparents), "I'd like to live with you always. Always!"

This fantasy of stepping into someone else's already running household is a familiar Jarrell ingredient. Only hinted at in "A Sick Child" (who wants some beings from another planet to come to him), it is fully developed in "Windows" where a man on a snowy sidewalk looks through the living room window of a lighted house and longs to be there with the woman who is darning while her husband nods in his chair. In his loneliness the man thinks of entering through one of the many windows and that

> Some morning they will come downstairs and find me.
> They will start to speak, and then smile speechlessly,
> Shifting the plates, set another place
> At a table shining by a silent fire.
> When I have eaten they will say, "You will have not slept."
> And from the sofa, mounded in my quilt,
>
> My face on *their* pillow, that is always cool,
> I will look up speechlessly into a—
>
> It blurs, and there is drawn across my face
> As my eyes close, a hand's slow fire-warmed flesh.

Later, in his novel *Pictures from an Institution* the innocent and guileless girl student at Benton College is, in the end, adopted by the childless Rosenbaums, a professor and his wife.

5

Here, too, the author irresistibly intervenes in the story, asking them, "Aren't you going to adopt me, too?" Again, in the end of Jarrell's children's book *The Animal Family*, the boy washed ashore on the island is adopted by the hunter and the mermaid.

The Gingerbread Rabbit—a book where the animals talk— is the natural outcome of a writer whose favorite juvenile reading (along with Hawthorne's *Tanglewood Tales*) included *Aesop's Fables*, *The Jungle Books*, and *Uncle Remus*. That the dialogue is the outstanding feature of the book is another natural outcome from a writer long used to treating dialogue as an art form in all his prose and poetry. Particularly exciting to a child are the seductive lies of the fox and menacing lines of the utensils as they make sport of the doughy rabbit spread on the kitchen table while the oven heats. They seem sufficiently entertaining in themselves, but are even more so if the parental reader can detect their parallels in the sinister "house" that talks in "A Quilt Pattern" and the wily Mephistopheles in *Faust*.

There is something else about *The Gingerbread Rabbit* that is not likely to be known by those outside the family. Jarrell endowed Mary's mother in the story with two distinctive characteristics of his own: his delight in giving and in surprising. A week rarely passed that he did not come up to one of us with anything (from the latest Schwartzkopf recording to a red star-shaped gum leaf) and happily give us the mock command:

> Open your hand,
> And close your eyes—
> And I'll give you something
> To make you wise,
> Surprise,
> *Surprise!*

Concerned primarily with the writing of this first children's book, Jarrell rather assumed that the writer found some illustrations he liked, told the editor about it, and the illustrator would come running. After leafing through more stacks of books on the low tables and in the little chairs, Jarrell found that Garth William's pen-and-ink drawings for the furry animals in Margery Sharp's *The Rescuers* were just what he wanted. Turning the matter over to di Capula, Jarrell had no idea of the difficult task he was setting for a very junior assistant editor at a very early stage in his career: to induce the established and much-in-demand illustrator of, among others, E. B. White's *Charlotte's Web* to add a first book by an unknown children's writer to his backlog. Di Capua kept to himself any qualms he had and concentrated his powers of persuasion on winning Williams over. That done, di Capua became an accomplished go-between for the two older artists—one in North Carolina, one in Mexico—who never had any direct personal contact with each other.

So it was that in July of 1962 Jarrell sent di Capua—to relay to Williams—a letter of guidance, saying:

> I'll write out a few things about the characters in *The Gingerbread Rabbit* and the most likely things to illustrate. The rabbit himself ought to be very sincere and naive and ingenuous, so that his whole body and face express what he feels. The big rabbit ought to be handsome, secure and competent-looking; the mother rabbit should be delicate and demure and beautiful. The fox should be very smooth and flashy, like Valentino playing W. C. Fields. The little girl's mother should be young (28 or so) and beautiful and kind, just the mother a little girl would want; the little girl should be something any little girl can immediately identify with.

Eight months later, in March 1963, Jarrell wrote di Capua: "I am delighted with the drawings: the gingerbread rabbit's *very* cute and touching. The fox is wonderful, and the old rabbit in the colored sketch makes me want to be adopted by him. . . . I believe Williams is getting quite inspired and will make a charming book."

After some astute inquiries from di Capua about what he would write next for children, Jarrell explained how he was busy preparing a formal lecture for the National Poetry Festival in Washington to be called "Fifty Years of American Poetry" and writing anthology introductions for Kipling and a volume of Russian Literature. "But I'm sure I can do some more things for children during the winter and spring," he wrote. "Doing them is a *great* pleasure and, so far, I don't have any of the trouble with them I have with grown-up things—may Heaven help me in that state always!"

II

By November, as Jarrell had hoped, he was able to start another book. He later described it to Aaron Kramer as:

> a book half for children, half for grown-ups called *The Bat-Poet* and that felt just like a regular book to me. And, you know how it is, you work on it all the time. You stay awake thinking about it at night. You wake up in the middle of the night . . . and, I did it just like a grown-up book. By good luck, we have some bats on our porch. I think they like the insects that come to the porchlight. And anyway, there really was one bat that was a different color from the rest. He was a kind of café-au-lait brown and I made him the Bat-Poet. And so I imagined a bat who could not *write* poems, but who would make them up; and so I had to make up poems for him. And a couple of the poems ["The Mockingbird" and "The Chipmunk's Day"] were pretty much like grown-up poems—anyway, the *New Yorker* printed them. I didn't tell them they were children's poems.

The story the grown-ups hear when they read *The Bat-Poet*

8

to their children is the allegory of the artist who, in Goethe's words, has "two hearts in one breast." They find, through the bat, not only his poet's heart that dares to turn from the conventional world to a self-invented one, but also his creature's heart that is lonely for his fellows to share in his world of art and imagination. But are his fellow bats ready to enter into, or even hear about, a foreign country with abrasive sounds and highly evolved monsters and charged with an incomprehensible dimension called Color? No! They are afraid and, though they are polite, they flee from the bat as a dubious and eccentric character. While the bat tries to resign himself to their indifference and to enjoy his reception among strangers, the time comes when he, too, must hibernate as the other bats have done already. The happy ending for him is that he was able to write a poem (not about the daylight world, but about bats) and that his new friend (the chipmunk) says the bats are *sure* to like it "the way I like the one about me."

The story the children usually hear is a simpler one, a story more explicitly concerned with a bat who writes poetry. His friend, a practical-minded chipmunk who likes the bat, tags these poems "portraits in verse" as he markets them in the natural world.

On the other hand, this book ("half for grown-ups and half for children") is really for artists: that is, the book tells the rest of the world what it is like for a tiny percentage to want to be part of the whole—not isolated; to communicate with the great world through literature, painting, music and the other arts; and finally, to make the world understand that art for the artist is more than turning on the spigot.

A good example of this occurs when the bat is unable to compose a poem about the cardinal. Since the bat had no difficulty writing about the mockingbird, the chipmunk, and the owl, it might be assumed he could write about the cardinal—

especially since he admired the cardinal and was interested in him. It was puzzling to the chipmunk that the bat could not; for that matter, it puzzled the bat; but no matter how much he wanted to do the cardinal's portrait, his vision failed him. This minor episode in the story came from Jarrell's attempt to write a book on Hart Crane for Holt and Company. Although Jarrell admired Crane, was extremely interested in him and had accepted a $2000 advance to write about him, he could not. After struggling more than a year with notes on Crane, and after spending the advance, Jarrell had to admit, as the bat did, "I would if I could, but I can't. I don't know why I can't, but I can't." And in Jarrell's case he had to struggle even further to pay back the advance.

Of the four portraits the bat accomplished, "Mockingbird" was Jarrell's favorite and he placed it second in his table of contents for his later book *The Lost World*. Under its Wordsworthian surface and its Yeatsian conclusion, the "Mockingbird" is a caricature drawn from Jarrell's knowledge of Lowell's and Frost's (*and his own*) self-obsession, acute sensitivity, and fierce territoriality. Through this poem he is pleading for the world to see that these are part of the cost of being "a real artist"—but a negligible part and a pardonable one when compared with the mockingbird in his best moments, when he achieves his unsurpassable imitations of life that make us pause, look up from what we are doing and say, "He's right. That's the way it really is."

The bat-poet, himself, has just this effect on the chipmunk in his portrait of the owl, "The Bird of Night." Jarrell based the poem on a barred owl we knew, one that hooted and hunted in our woods. Although the owl is first presented visually, it is plain, suddenly, one is hearing the owl, too. In a subtle onomatopoeia Jarrell creates (out of repetitive *l*'s and *w*'s and legato vowels) the stir of air when a sizable feathered object glides through it downward, and more downward to seize its prey. This imitation of life was so real to the chipmunk that he shivered at the end and said, "It's terrible, just terrible! . . . I'm going to bed earlier. Sometimes when there're lots of nuts I stay out till it's pretty dark; but believe me, I'm never going to again."

The chipmunk sat twice for his portrait. Once he is depicted in verse—also onomatopoeic—by means of short, staccato words and lines and the musicality of o and e sounds punctuated with sharp t's. This portrays him as a neat, fleet body darting through its days, content at sunset to have fed himself and escaped the talons of the owl. His prose portrait was a character study revealing him as the bat's devoted friend, loyal supporter, and able entrepreneur. This I recognized—and Jarrell admitted laughingly—was a sort of tribute to di Capua and myself.

The facts for the family portrait "Bats" were gleaned from Jarrell's reading about their mammalian birthing and suckling behavior and was modified by his summer-long observation of the vulnerable little colony bunched upside-down by our porch light. By now quite fond of the bats, Jarrell approached the poem in a lyrical way, and somewhat transformed their homely truths into such lines as these:

> A bat is born
> Naked and blind and pale.
> His mother makes a pocket of her tail
> And catches him. He clings to her long fur
> By his thumbs and toes and teeth.
> And then the mother dances through the night
> Doubling and looping, soaring, somersaulting—
> Her baby hangs on underneath
> All night, in happiness, she hunts and flies.
>
> . . . .
>
> Her baby drinks the milk she makes him
> In moonlight or starlight, in mid-air.

11

Their single shadow, printed on the moon
Or fluttering across the stars,
Whirls on all night . . .

Jarrell simply assumed Garth Williams would do the illustrations for *The Bat-Poet*. So absorbed in the new poems he was able to write, Jarrell had not given the illustrator a second thought: but di Capua had. Di Capua had his eye on young Maurice Sendak who was a versatile and original artist with a growing reputation, who had his own bestseller at Harper's (*The Nutshell Library*), and who was, furthermore, a Grimm's enthusiast! Di Capua proposed Sendak for *The Bat-Poet* and in the future for an expanded volume of Grimm's tales to be translated by Jarrell.

At first this was a jolt: Sendak was not a household word in North Carolina and Williams was—in our household at least, especially due to his association with *The New Yorker* writer E. B. White. This time di Capua focused his powers of persuasion on Jarrell, and after another stint in the little chairs at the low tables Jarrell was able to write him, "[On seeing] nine or ten Sendak books and five or six more of Garth Williams' books, I feel as you do about Sendak. He's better at lyric or quiet or thoughtful or imaginative effects. . . . I liked many of his animals—his bear family, for instance—very much. He would probably be better for the tone of *The Bat-Poet*." Thus, the decision was made.

In a "Dear Mr. Sendak" letter of February 1963, Jarrell said: "I've almost no suggestions and want you to do it just as it comes to you. The animals like the mockingbird and chipmunk are very much the same as the real ones, so color photographs or watching the real animals might help you. That particular sort of little brown bat, on the other hand, has too much a devil's face to use; other sorts of bat, just bats for instance, have faces more like squirrels' or mice's and you could invent a face for him

12

more like theirs." Jarrell closed with, "We had an awfully good time at your house after the Opera; I hope you can come visit us sometime. In the spring the bats, the chipmunk, the mocking-bird and the cardinal are all right here."

Though Sendak was not able to visit the bat-poet's home, he was able—by some inexplicable empathy—to duplicate, almost, the exact corner and woodwork and light on our porch where the bats clustered. Further on in the book he again, coincidentally, illustrated an uncanny likeness in the wooded scene with the old-fashioned bench to our own mossy, wild side garden.

When Jarrell saw the finished book he wrote di Capua: "I (Mary, too) was really *enchanted* with the look of *The Bat-Poet*. It's exactly right, I think; it even has a sort of serious, elevated look as if it were a classic, as much for grown-ups as for children. I think Maurice did it wonderfully. The printing and the paper are perfect. I'm crazy about the small bat drawings at the side (of the pages) the ones he (added) at the last; some of them are the most accomplished drawings of bats I've ever seen."

Jarrell was also pleased with his own part of *The Bat-Poet* and said in the Kramer interview, "I've been awfully happy about what readers have said to me and what I've read in the reviews. You know sometimes you feel you have good *luck* with a book. Things *come* to you. And I feel that way about it, . . . that *The Bat-Poet,* for what it is, *is* done right."

III

Having written the four poems for *The Bat-Poet*, Jarrell wrote twenty more during the next two years which made possible his last book of poetry, *The Lost World*. At the same time he was writing not one, but two children's stories: *The Animal Family* which di Capua took with him when he left Macmillan for Pantheon, and *Fly by Night* which di Capua took with him to Farrar, Straus and Giroux.

The very first intimation of *The Animal Family* as a book dates back to 1951 when Jarrell was teaching at Princeton, getting divorced, and trying to keep house alone. In November of that year he wrote me in Laguna, California: "I think I'm going to write a poem rather like 'Deutsch Durch Freud' called 'The Poet-Cook'; at least, I've been thinking about it. I'll have a mermaid in it that comes to live with the Hero. I've already thought of some details like little pools of water where she stands, [and] the flop of her tail as she comes up the stairs. In some ways she's going to be like another mermaid I know—I bet nobody's ever written a poem about a poet-cook with a mermaid. Ah, originality!" Actually, Jarrell's novel (*Pictures from an Institution*) took immediate precedence over this poem, and there were other attractive options. Twelve years went by before he thought of the mermaid and the Hero again: but not as a poem. This time the little pools of water and the flop of the mermaid's tail went into a story and the Hero was not a poet-cook, but a hunter, and they all made a book called *The Animal Family*.

This joyous tale is about a Garden of Eden without the Expulsion; and it took place—in Jarrell's mind—partly along a wild shoreline "where the forest runs down to the sea" which he had seen in Oregon one summer and in a cove near Seal Rocks where we swam with Catalina Island on the horizon. In the story the hunter's house was built by his own hands, but his deerskin rugs really came out of our own house and had been bought in Salzburg. Likewise, "the big brass horn he had found in a wreck" was one we found at Gucci's in Florence and hung over our mantel. And the ship's figurehead that the mermaid brought up from the sea was based on a charming lead figure Jarrell had bought from an antique dealer in Amsterdam. Its description in the book is entirely accurate: "a woman with bare breasts and fair hair, who clasped her hands behind her head; she wore a necklace of tiny blue flowers, and had a garland of big flowers around her thighs. But her legs and feet weren't a woman's at all, but the furry, delicate, sharp-hooved legs of a deer or goat—and they were crossed at the ankles."

The characters in *The Animal Family* were composites, of course, modeled on fact and fantasy. The hunter was created out of the part of Jarrell that had a beard and a fur hat made of coon-tails; the part that still wanted to play with bows and arrows; and the part that fondly identified with Orion, the hunter constellation. In a letter in 1943 to his first wife, written from an airfield in Arizona, Jarrell described the night sky outside his tent as "extremely beautiful, and old Orion, my mascot (I'm convinced God made him for me) looks as H. G. Wells-ish as ever." Later "The Hunter's" starry belt and sword appeared in two poems, the novel, and a piece of criticism.

The mermaid of the Animal Family was Jarrell's ideal of a beautiful consort who, for love of him, would forsake her family and friends, learn a new and intellectual language, be dear and funny always, put him first, and never turn into a Wife or Mother.

Their silver-furred and silver-eyed lynx was, from the outside, a replica of the Canadian lynx in the Washington Zoo whom we furtively fed with bits of liver and duckskin when we lived in Chevy Chase. Underneath, however, the lynx was Jarrell's cat of many years, Kitten; and he was given Kitten's attributes—"delicate," "deft," "quick," and "clever." When the lynx kneads his paws on the chamois shirts or pounces on a ball or stretches out flat on his outstretched paws watching, thinking, and dozing, Jarrell is commemorating this beloved cat. The bear was brought in for comic relief and because Jarrell had a wish-fantasy about owning a bear. And the boy joined them to complete the archetypal family, to satisfy the hunter's troubled longing for continuity and to esthetically round the circle that began when the hunter as a little boy was shipwrecked on the island.

The Animal Family was so directly inspired by the rocky coastline, the blue and white surf, and the infinitude of sky on the westward edge of our continent, that Jarrell thought nothing but nature photography would suit the story. After reading it, Sendak said it was an impossible one for him to illustrate, that "the images are so graphically created in the writing that Jarrell does not need me." As Sendak enthusiasts well know, his first principle is that illustrations must amplify the text and not duplicate it, and the vivid writing in this passage of Jarrell's is typical of what Sendak was up against: "In spring the meadow that ran down from the cliff to the beach was all foam-white and sea-blue with flowers; the hunter looked at it and it was beautiful. . . . And when at evening, past the dark blue shape of a far-off island, the sun sank under the edge of the sea like a red world vanishing, the hunter saw it all, but there was no one to tell what he had seen."

Jarrell and I began searching through Ansel Adams and Edward Weston albums of western photography, and Jarrell wrote di Capua to see what he could find in the New York Public Library. What he wanted, Jarrell said, was: "1) The coast seen from out at sea. 2) The normal view of the beach, with the surf, the meadow, and the mountains. 3) The view from above that the hunter and the mermaid see in the last scene, just before they go into the cabin."

Sendak was appealed to when nothing usable came out of our search, but he still maintained the impossibility of his illustrating such a book as *The Animal Family*. Jarrell knew what Sendak meant and was dismayed; di Capua knew, too, but for Jarrell's sake determinedly (but diplomatically) persuaded Sendak to "decorate" the book instead of "illustrating" it.

The seven black-and-white landscapes Sendak drew to separate and introduce the chapters are pure "Sendakland." Of these, Jarrell's favorite was the romantic decoration for the courtship chapter between the hunter and the mermaid where Sendak created a moonlit seascape under a baroque sky with some Mozart wafted on the breeze. Then follows a startling departure from Jarrell's Paradise in Sendak's scene for chapter 3 which seems to depict a rough-hewn block of granite with graveyard overtones imbedded among—and hovered over by—some gnarled and ancient arterial system. Nowhere does Sendak personify the humans and animals in the family; however, a tiny cabin that can be easily overlooked is at the base of his lion-pawed cliffs in the opening chapter, implying the family's habitation just as the bow and arrows tossed into the tree in the final chapter imply the presence, somewhere, of a boy.

In September of 1965, Jarrell wrote:

Dear Maurice: I feel so lucky and grateful to have had your pictures for both *The Animal Family* and *The Bat-Poet*. *The Animal Family* was harder for you, since you couldn't make the pictures direct illustrations and since the drawing came right in the middle of such a hard time for you [Sendak's father had been seriously ill]. . . . I'm so grateful to you for working so hard on them and making them so beautiful. It's hard for me to pick the ones I like best—the one of the moonlight on the sea and the dustjacket itself are my favorites, almost. It will make so much difference to readers having your decorations rather than a book with drawings—the book will feel rich and full to them in a way it couldn't possibly without what you've done. They really are some of your most original and profound drawings—not only will readers of *The Animal Family* love them, but there are all the people who get any book you make the drawings for, just because they're your drawings.

As mentioned previously, the writing of *The Animal Family* as well as *Fly by Night* was done in Jarrell's time off from writing his long autobiographical quartet called "The Lost World." Compared with writing poetry, this prose came so smoothly it scarcely needed any revision. Handwritten in black ink on unlined typing paper, *The Animal Family* poured through Jarrell faster than he could legibly write it. The family he created, for the woods and meadows by the sea, knew nothing of disease, nor depression—emotional or financial; and no one in it was critical, competitive or mean. The grown-ups never argued, just talked about their childhoods, gave each other presents, joked, and sat together in their doorway—a hunter, and a mermaid, with a bear and a boy, watching a lynx trot over the sand "far along the beach by a little river."

IV

Jarrell had also sent Sendak a letter about the other children's book: "For the last three weeks I've been writing an owl's bedtime story in *terza rima*. It's more or less the climax of the book. This new book—it's a sort of dream book, all in the present tense—is named *Fly by Night*. This poem, "The Owl's Bedtime Story," featured the same barred owl that appeared in *The Bat-Poet*. We had found its daytime roost in a dark part of our woods. For several days we visited the owl, seating ourselves on the pine needles and peering up at it to marvel at the camouflaging rings around its body and the almost mechanistic circles surrounding its eyes. When it gave up trying to sleep there we never saw it again, though we occasionally heard it at night and would wake up and murmur, "Our owl." The poem belongs in the last of Jarrell's nature phase, and the boy dreaming he could fly was a surplus memory from Jarrell's childhood that he had not put into the poem quartet "The Lost World."

In "The Owl's Bedtime Story" a lonely owlet waits in a hollow tree and thinks to himself, "Come home! Come home!" when his mother is off hunting (as Jarrell's mother used to be off working). After awhile, the owlet gets the courage to try his wings by day to rescue (adopt) an orphaned owlet whose cries he has heard. In the end, the "good" mother brings the nestlings things to eat and "when she opened her wings, they nestled to her breast."

David, the boy in the story, could fly by night and was lonely, too, in his hollow room down the hall, cut off from his parents. In his dream of flying—"really, he is floating"—David sees his mother and associates her with pancakes for breakfast, sees his father and associates him with Oedipal rivalry, and then floats out of the house to observe some mice below him and then some rabbits, sheep and ponies. In classic dream tradition, David is given a dreamer's omniscient overview and the familiar paralysis (he is unable to speak or act). Contrarily, Jarrell gave him no stress or anxiety—only a kind of puzzled wonder. Never stating this—or anything else—with intensity, Jarrell then steers the floating boy back to the security of his blanket where David "starts to fall asleep." The book ends in the daylight of the sunny kitchen where David's mother kisses him with a loving look "like . . . like?" Like the look of the mother owl, but that instantly dissolves into his own mother's look and she says to him, "In two shakes of a lamb's tail I'll have some pancakes ready for you."

Jarrell wrote Sendak concerning the pictures for *Fly by Night:* the book "will be so easy for you to illustrate that I've laughed over the thought again and again. . . . Paragraph by paragraph it divides into pictures, and pictures thoroughly in your own style." While Jarrell had reached back into his own boyhood for the story, Sendak reached back into nineteenth-century England for the pictures and there, in a pastoral Hardyish countryside, Sendak rendered the late twilight and deep night that the nude, sleeping boy floated through.

In all his books for children, Jarrell minded the golden rule that insists on a happy ending and he did this in his dream-book in double measure: once at the conclusion of "The Owl's Bedtime Story" and then again in the finale of *Fly by Night* itself. With only one main character and hardly any plot, Jarrell made the technical challenge of this book the portrayal of a dream-state as much as that of a dream's contents.

Actually, he often employed dreams as a fifth dimension and for years had used the dream-device in poems as a way of entering the unconscious of his soldiers, women, and children; and more than once Jarrell's dead speak through dreams. Scholars consistently list "Dreams" as one of his six literary subjects and, in fact, four of Jarrell's poems have the word dream in the title and more than thirty of them are—or are about—dreams. Minute, but typical is the allusion in "The Death of the Ball Turret Gunner" where, hunched in the belly of the fighter plane, the gunner is "Six miles from earth, loosed from its dream of life." Dreams frequently came to his aid for a lyric or satiric metaphor in his criticism or as a mine for hidden truths about a character (e.g., Gertrude's in *Pictures from an Institution* or, more pertinently, the hunter's in *The Animal Family*). Considering this, it is hardly surprising that Jarrell found the idea of creating a book-length dream irresistible and that, having got David's dream underway, made up one for David's mother, father, dog, and a whole flock of sheep—where Jarrell joked, "All of them except one are dreaming they're eating; that one is dreaming he's asleep."

Jarrell and Sendak know, as you and I know, that "flying" has a sexual connotation and that such words as pancakes, fur, rings, panting, and mice have, for the Freudian initiate, an erotic charge; but the triumph of this book is that David knows

20

none of this at all. Through Jarrell's delicate rhetoric and his sensitive tone, *Fly by Night* is a tranquil improvisation on the dream-technique of tentative suggestion and elaborate disguise.

V

In a letter to Sendak in 1965 Jarrell said: "I'm hoping so to write a new children's story now . . . and to have the marvelous thrill of seeing your illustrations for it," but in less than a month he was struck by a car and killed. Randall Jarrell's books for children, however, have lived on in the years since then. All four are in print, *The Animal Family* is a Newberry Honor Book, and each one has been translated into French or German or Japanese or Hebrew.

Garth Williams, Jarrell's first illustrator, after a distinguished career, is now retired and living in New Mexico. Maurice Sendak is not in the least retired but is living busily in his home in Connecticut. Having won both Caldecott Awards and Medals, designed costumes and sets for a number of operas (including *The Magic Flute, The Nutcracker Suite,* and his own *Where the Wild Things Are*), Sendak is now considering film-making.

Over the years, Jarrell's editor, Michael di Capua, has brought out *Fly by Night;* four of Jarrell's grown-up books; and invented, in a manner of speaking, the edition (which won the Caldecott Award) of Jarrell's translation of *Snow-White* with the superb illustrations of Nancy Eckholm Burkert, and the edition of *The Fisherman's Wife* illustrated by Margot Zemach. Finally, di Capua accomplished his long-hoped-for edition of Grimm's tales (*The Juniper Tree*) using four translations by Jarrell and the rest by Lore Segal, and entirely illustrated by Sendak. In the years since I first read Jarrell the query on Macmillan stationary from an unknown beginner in publishing, di Capua has steadily moved upward until, today, he is editor-in-chief and a vice-president at Farrar, Straus and Giroux; and while he seems to have worked on his last Jarrell book—but who knows what he might instigate?—a photograph of his bearded and unforgotten friend still graces his office wall.

Chapter One

THE
GINGERBREAD RABBIT

In November of 1962, Jarrell wrote Robert Penn Warren: "I translated some German fairy tales for a nice children's editor, Michael di Capua, and before I knew it I'd written a children's book too. . . . It feels queer and entertaining to write a sort of thing you've never written before."[1] Jarrell's first children's book, *The Gingerbread Rabbit,* grew out of his work for di Capua: it is a modern fairy tale, one in which he supplies a happy ending for the folk tale "The Gingerbread Boy."

Jarrell found in Garth Williams a sympathetic illustrator for his story. Williams had illustrated *Little House in the Big Woods* (1953) and other books in this series by Laura Ingalls Wilder—stories that, like Jarrell's, combine the domesticity of the house with the wildness of the woods. Moreover, Williams had shown himself skilled at drawing small creatures when illustrating George Thompson's *A Cricket in Times Square* (1960), and Margery Sharp's mice in *The Rescuers* (1959) and *Miss Bianca* (1962). But the pictures in *The Gingerbread Rabbit* most recall Williams's famous illustrations for E. B. White's *Charlotte's Web* (1952)—perhaps because the stories are similar: both the gingerbread rabbit and Wilbur the pig are concerned

23

about being eaten and, through the comradeship of other animals, find a way of not being invited for dinner.

The original folktale tells of an old man and woman who wish for a child and about the old woman preparing a gingerbread boy who runs away just as he is about to be popped into the oven; he runs away from quite a few others and taunts each of them with a ditty that builds to his final boast:

> I've run away from a little old woman,
> A little old man,
> A barn full of threshers,
> A field full of mowers,
> A cow and a pig,
> And I can run away from you, I can!

In the end, the gingerbread creature has his comeuppance when he arrives at a river and a fox helps him across; as the water gets deeper, the fox tells the creature to climb on his tail, then higher until he finally reaches the fox's nose where, with a tip of the head, the fox makes a meal of him.

Jarrell's story shares a number of motifs with the folktale: the gingerbread creature and the fox, an old couple's wish for a child, the oven, the escape, and the chase. The differences, however, are more significant. For reasons of his own, yet to be explained, Jarrell changes the gingerbread boy into a gingerbread rabbit. Jarrell also changes the conclusion.

The folk tale's conclusion is an abrupt one that points to a moral (pride goes before the fall) but far from the happy ending readers have come to expect in children's stories. In this, it resembles Charles Perrault's seventeenth-century version of "Little Red Riding Hood" which has its own moral (don't talk to wolfish strangers) and ends abruptly with Little Red being eaten by the wolf. Subsequent storytellers were dissatisfied with Perrault's conclusion, and over the years reshaped "Little Red Riding Hood" until the oral version collected by the Grimm brothers two centuries later ends with the chastened little girl being retrieved from the wolf by cesarean surgery. In a similar fashion, Jarrell reworks "The Gingerbread Boy" to finish it with a happy ending.

Jarrell's story presented his illustrator with a number of challenges. Williams's most formidable task lay in picturing the gingerbread rabbit itself. That character was, after all, a cookie, a doughboy. Still, the creature had to be animate and show such feelings as terror and innocence. Worst of all, this doughy creature was mobile. Williams had some suggestions in the text (the rabbit would "roll over and over like a wheel with six spokes") but the pictorial solutions were his own (Figure 1).

The dynamism of Jarrell's text presented Williams with other problems. The book is one of almost constant motion— the rabbit's escape, the mother's hunt through the woods, the chase by the fox, etc. Williams's solution was twofold. In some cases, he portrayed change from one picture to another: Mary's mother, for example, is a well-groomed Jacqueline Kennedy look-alike as the story opens (Figure 2) but by the time her frenetic search is underway she is bedraggled and unkempt with exertion.

In other situations, Williams illustrated Jarrell's dynamism in double-page spreads. The mother's pursuit of the rabbit, for example, begins on a path on a left-hand page and then spills over to the right-hand page before curling back on to the other once again. Likewise, the fox's chase is presented by a scurrying fox on an upper part of a left page in pursuit of the rabbit pair who are hurrying off a lower part of the right page (Figure 3).

Perhaps what is unique about Williams' pictorial style can be easily understood if *The Gingerbread Rabbit* is considered in terms of another rabbit story—Beatrix Potter's *The Tale of Peter Rabbit*. Unlike Potter's more static watercolor cameos,

Figure 1

Figure 2

and just two steps behind, his long tail switch-
ing and his big teeth shining, came the fox.
But the big rabbit could run a lot faster than
the fox, and the gingerbread rabbit, now that
he'd got all rested again, could run faster than
anything—the two of them got farther and
farther ahead of the fox, until finally they
couldn't even see him or hear him any more.

Figure 3

And then they came to a little stream that ran
between the forest and a meadow, and instead
of jumping across, the big brown rabbit said:
"Over here!" They ran along the bank for a
few steps. There at the edge of the water,
under a willow tree with rushes and watercress
growing all around it, was a little shady round

Williams's pen-and-ink sketches properly reflect the hurried-ness of Jarrell's text. And while Potter presents her personified creatures through abundant accoutrements from waistcoats and shoes to thatched baskets, Williams (perhaps because he was working with a story which already had an anthropomorphic cookie creature) presents his animals with only a few props (the fatherly rabbit smokes a pipe) and more through posture (the wily fox winking and confiding with his arm around the gullible gingerbread rabbit, Figure 4). These are just the right touch.

I

In a fashion, the title itself suggests an entrance into the meaning and origins of the story. The "rabbit" recalls an incident from Jarrell's childhood that he was to recount in "The Lost World" and other poems: how he had been bewildered when "Mama," his loving grandmother, had wrung a chicken's neck and how he had wondered if she might do the same to his pet rabbit. The "gingerbread" of the title not only recalls "The Gingerbread Boy," but also the gingerbread house in the Grimm's "Hansel and Gretel"; and when Jarrell made use of this fairy tale in his poem "A Quilt Pattern," he wrote of a boy who dreamed he was a rabbit held, like Hansel, in a cage.

The Gingerbread Rabbit shares a number of images with the Grimm tale: the fearsome woods, the ogreish deceiver, the oven and the kneading of dough. But Jarrell's story comes closest to "Hansel and Gretel" in its accentuation of issues of orality—its preoccupation with eating and the fear of being eaten.

Jarrell's book opens with a mother who wishes to make a surprise for her daughter Mary who is away at school. She decides, after she sees a rabbit in the woods, that she will make a gingerbread rabbit. As the woman prepares her surprise, something occurs which might otherwise seem insignificant except

30

Figure 4

for later events in the story: "It all smelled so good the mother couldn't keep from licking the spoon" (2).

When a vegetable man calls out his wares, the mother leaves the kitchen for a few minutes and the gingerbread rabbit comes to life. He immediately asks where and who he is, and the kitchen implements respond:

> Here in the kitchen, . . . where they cook you and eat you . . . because you're a rabbit, . . . an animal that lives in the forest, . . . and whenever anyone comes near he runs away, because he's afraid they'll shoot him and eat him. . . . Not you. . . . You're only a gingerbread rabbit. They'll put you in the oven and bake you. . . . Bake you and eat you! . . . They eat them all the time. . . . The woman eats them all the time, and her husband eats them, and her little girl eats them. Everything that comes into the kitchen they eat. (6–10)

Like the child hero in "Jack and the Beanstalk" who finds himself in the giant's kitchen, the gingerbread rabbit realizes the danger he is in and (taking a cue from the behavior of real rabbits) runs away when the woman returns from her errand—especially because he notes that "there in the middle of her face were dozens of tremendous shining white teeth the size of a grizzly bear's" (12). Like Jack's giant, the mother gives chase.

Orality is also an issue when the gingerbread rabbit flees into the woods, meets a squirrel, but has to continue his flight because the squirrel is unable to lift him into the security of its nest. Having been told by the rabbit that a "giant" is in pursuit, the squirrel is confused when he hears the "giant" crying and discovers it is only the kindly woman who feeds him nuts. The squirrel explains the confusion: "He [the gingerbread rabbit] thinks you're going to eat him. To cook and eat him" (24). The mother protests: "I wouldn't dream of eating him now. I want him to be a pet for my little girl. . . . Why, of course, I won't eat him. . . . Do you think I'm a *cannibal*?" (26). The mother's statement, needless to say, is strange, not only because of the revelatory addition of "now," but because her overly dramatic abhorrence of carnivorous behavior would be a slender consolation to a rabbit made of vegetable matter.

Oral threats are also present when the rabbit next encounters a fox. A cousin to the deceptive wolf in "Little Red Riding Hood," the fox claims that he, too, is a rabbit—albeit a "red rabbit." When the gingerbread creature confides his tale of woe, the fox explodes in mock horror: "'*Eat* you!' cried the other. 'Eat *you!* But who could be guilty of such an enormity? I myself have been, for almost more years than I can remember, a vegetarian; but the thought that even the most confirmed meat-eater could bear to gobble up so young, so innocent, so tender a rabbit as yourself . . .'—he brushed a tear out of his eyes, swallowed, and licked his lips—'the thought is one that—the very thought of it is—why, my dear boy, words fail me!'" (28). Like Little Red Riding Hood who gullibly accepts the wolf-in-gramma's-clothing, the innocent gingerbread rabbit accepts the fox when he claims to be a rabbit himself but also notes what big teeth his companion has.

Just as he is about to take sanctuary in the fox's cave (and meet his certain doom), the gingerbread rabbit hears a scampering in the forest. It is another rabbit (a real, brown one) who balks at the gingerbread creature's invitation to escape from the ogreish "giant" by hiding in the cave of this "red rabbit." Sizing up the fox for what he is, the brown rabbit seizes the gingerbread youngster and carries him away in a pell-mell escape from the conniving carnivore.

Orality appears in a more positive light when the real rabbit takes the gingerbread version to a snug hole where he and his wife have their home. They have already prepared three beds: "We have always wanted a little rabbit of our own" (42–43), the old couple explains; and their gingerbread kin happily agrees to adoption. Fears of being consumed disappear as the real rabbits feed tiny carrots to their new son; and he discovers that he prefers eating to being eaten.

Food continues to be an issue elsewhere in the woods when the mother encounters the fox and the woman inquires about her gingerbread rabbit: "The fox said: 'What's gingerbread?' 'Well,' said the mother, 'it's what you get when you mix together flour and molasses and brown sugar and ginger, and then bake them all in the oven.' 'What does it taste like?' asked the fox. 'Meat?' 'Oh, no,' said the mother. 'It's more like vegetables.' 'Vegetables!' exclaimed the fox. 'To think that I got all out of breath running after a vegetable!'" (45). The mother explains that she intended to make the creature a pet for her daughter and, lacking one, offers the position to the fox. Only one thing is important to him: when the woman answers that he will be fed dog food, the fox declines the offer.

Finally (as if recalling Margery Bianco's *The Velveteen Rabbit*), the mother realizes she would have less trouble if she made her daughter a sewn rabbit and heads home to do so. When little Mary returns from school, she is surprised and delighted to find a cloth rabbit that looks so much like a gingerbread one and like a real one. And because this one is not edible, Mary's mother can assure her that this one won't "run right off into the forest" (53).

In the nights which follow, while Mary nestles in her bed with her cloth rabbit and sleeps, the gingerbread rabbit comes with his new parents to the edge of the forest. On his way to the carrot or turnip patch, he often looks at the house of the "giant" and shudders to remember, "Oh, those teeth! Did she almost cook me! Did she almost eat me!" (53). Though his rabbit-parents know it is only a mother and her daughter, they are amused by their son's notion of a boogie and indulge him and run away together in mock terror.

II

Like "Hansel and Gretel," *The Gingerbread Rabbit* is story full of issues of orality. Like the fairy tale, too, Jarrell's story associates the threat of oral destruction with a maternal figure.[2] For this reason, there is more than meets the eye in the rabbit-parents' opinion that "it wasn't a giant at all, but just a mother" (55).

In his poem "The Lost World," Jarrell described a significant event in his childhood. At the time, the eleven-year-old boy was living with his grandparents in Hollywood and had a pet rabbit named "Reddy." In the poem a young Jarrell watches as his grandmother ("Mama") comes into the backyard:

> Mama comes out and takes in the clothes
> From the clothesline. She looks with righteous love
> At all of us, her spare face half a girl's.
> She enters a chicken coop, and the hens shove
> And flap and squawk, in fear; the whole flock whirls
> Into the farthest corner. She chooses one,
> Comes out, and wrings its neck. The body hurls
> Itself out—lunging, reeling, it begins to run
> Away from Something, to fly away from Something
> In great flopping circles. Mama stands like a nun
> In the center of the awful, anguished ring.
> The thudding and scrambling go on, go on—then they fade,
> I open my eyes, it's over . . . Could such a thing
> Happen to anything? It could happen to a rabbit, I'm afraid;
> It could to—

In the original manuscript for the poem in the New York Public

Library, what follows the dash is Jarrell's penciled-in conclusion: "it could happen to Randall, I'm afraid."

Bewildered by this childhood discovery—how Mama could be both loving and threatening—the young child turns to his grandmother and apprehensively inquires about his own safety as much as that of his pet rabbit Reddy:

> "Mama, you won't kill Reddy ever,
> You won't ever, will you?" The farm woman tries to persuade
> The little boy, her grandson, that she'd never
> Kill the boy's rabbit, never even think of it.
> He would like to believe her . . . And whenever
> I see her, there in that dark infinite,
> Standing like Judith, with the hen's head in her hand,
> I explain it away, in vain—a hypocrite,
> Like all who love. [3]

There are a number of motifs from this incident which reappear in *The Gingerbread Rabbit*, most notably the rabbit/child who feels endangered by a mother-figure. What may not be clear, however, is the relevance of the last lines of the poem to Jarrell's children's book—how he explains away and engages in loving hypocrisy when he thinks of "Mama" as a threatening figure. To understand that, we must turn to another poem.

Jarrell had earlier combined the two ingredients of *The Gingerbread Rabbit*—the story of "Hansel and Gretel" and the rabbit episode of his childhood—in his celebrated poem "A Quilt Pattern," where a boy falls asleep and re-dreams the fairy tale. What is worth noting is that the boy does not imagine himself as a Hansel held captive in a cage in the witch's yard, but as a caged rabbit. Like the gingerbread rabbit, like Hansel, this rabbit-boy feels he is in danger of being eaten by a woman. But what is most important in the poem is how the child steadfastly refuses to acknowledge that this threatening dream figure is his mother; he prevaricates—or in Jarrell's words, he explains it

36

away and engages in loving hypocrisy—and insists that this threatening figure is "the Other."

In the rabbit episode of his childhood, Jarrell encountered the puzzling fact that parents can be *both* loving and threatening. It is a confusing dilemma for all children: how can my mother or father be both the person who feeds me and the one who spanks me? What the child frequently concludes is that it cannot be the same person: there must be a Good Parent (who is my true mother or father) and a Bad Parent (to whom I am not related). In fairy tales like "Hansel and Gretel," there is the Good Mother and then there is the Other—the ogre-witch.

This phenomenon occurs in *The Gingerbread Rabbit*. In the early part of the book Mary's mother *seems* both loving and threatening. What actually exists, however, is a confusion on the part of the gingerbread rabbit: he feels endangered by the mother because he believes she intends to eat him, while the other creatures in the woods know she is a kind woman. Midway through the book Jarrell resolves this issue in the familiar childhood manner by splitting the mother into two parts: the Good Parents and the Other, the loving rabbit-couple and the threatening fox.

The link between the mother and the rabbit-couple is only suggested at first by the idea that they are all parents; and the benign aspect of the rabbits is suggested in their offer of adoption to the gingerbread creature: it will be "exactly the same as if you were our very own rabbit. We've always wanted to have a little rabbit of our own, and that is why we made the other little bed here" (42–43). But the identification is made clearer when Jarrell describes the mother's joy at coming up with the idea of making a sewn rabbit: she clapped her hands and "made a noise that sounded like a rabbit squealing, she was so overjoyed" (49).

If the rabbit-couple represents the loving side of the mother, then the fox represents her threatening side. The links between the mother and the fox are abundant: both are roaming the woods in pursuit of the gingerbread rabbit, and he flees both after noting their threatening teeth. Moreover, both the mother and the fox seem recent converts to vegetarianism; and if not that, then both deny their intentions of eating him though their actions indicate otherwise: despite his disavowals, the fox licks his lips when he thinks of the "tender" rabbit; and when the gingerbread rabbit is prepared, "it all smelled so good the mother couldn't help licking the spoon." And when it comes to denials, the mother, like the fox, doth protest too much.

Williams's picture of the meeting between the mother and the fox brilliantly indicates the link between them. They are posed in identical postures—one hand on the waist, the other on the rock they share. They are both weary, because both have been spending their day chasing the gingerbread rabbit; and, because they have both been engaged in the same fruitless activity, they sympathetically understand each other. Their relaxed posture and the contact between their eyes suggest they are confidantes. And the fact the mother's hair is unkempt, and that she has taken her shoe off, implies an unusual familiarity between them—as if to say, "Let's kick off our shoes and let our hair down" (Figure 5).

That Jarrell associates the threatening side of the mother with the masculine fox does not appear to have any special significance; like the wolf-in-gramma's-clothing in "Little Red Riding Hood," the folk tradition admits some plasticity in terms of gender. Instead, the split of the mother into rabbit-couple and fox can be described most accurately as following the conventional childhood split into Good Parent and Bad Parent. This dyad arises because children must discover a way to accommodate the confusing discovery that a parent can be both loving and threatening. It was this discovery which confused the young Randall Jarrell when he saw that his loving grandmother

38

Figure 5

was also a "Judith" who could wring a chicken's neck (as the Biblical Judith decapitated Holofernes). And this very same confusion is pictured by Williams on the cover of the book: in the foreground stands a puzzled gingerbread rabbit between his Good Parent and his Bad Parent—between the loving rabbit who walks with authority in the open air, and the threatening fox (with lolling tongue and averted eyes) who hides in the underbrush (Figure 6).

Looking back at his discovery that his grandmother was also a "Judith," Jarrell admits in "The Lost World" that he still engages in loving hypocrisy and explains it all away. The child who splits a parent into a Good and Bad figure is also engaged in extenuation. So, too, then, are the rabbit-parents who stand at the edge of the woods with their son and look at the house; they explain things away by thinking: "It wasn't a giant at all, but just a mother" (55).

There are some things children won't tell, and one of these is that they sometimes feel threatened by the parent who loves them. In taking up this fundamental childhood issue in *The Gingerbread Rabbit*, both author and illustrator go beyond the superficialities of everyday books for children to touch upon deeper truths.

III

More than 145,000 copies of *The Gingerbread Rabbit* are in print, quite an extraordinary number for a children's book. But despite the successes of the story and the accomplishments of the pictures, it is still the least satisfying of Jarrell's children's books. There are a number of reasons why this is so.

The success of a fantasy, that admixture of reality and imaginative possibility, depends upon a reader's "willing suspension of disbelief." As Margaret Blount (in her study of ani-

40

Figure 6

mals in children's fiction) and G. K. Chesterton (in his essay on fantasy) point out, a reader is prepared to accept many unrealistic things and to grant an author wide imaginative license under the proviso that the author be consistent with rules of logic (for example, two plus two must continue to equal four) and with rules of his or her own making (for example, if some of Aesop's animals are able to speak, then all animals possess this power).[4] To say this simply: in the world of the Grimm's fairy tales, a tree may bear golden apples; but when apples fall from that tree, they must fall *down*.

Jarrell is not completely successful in this fashion. To mention one thing, *The Gingerbread Rabbit* is the only one of his four children's books where inanimate things are given the power of speech, but in this regard Jarrell is inconsistent. The gingerbread creature is able to talk, and so are the paring knife and the mixing bowl and the rolling pin who lecture him in the kitchen. Why, then, isn't everything later (the trees in the forest or the fox's cave, for example) equally animate and loquacious?

Moreover, the accomplished fantasist employs unreality in an *a priori* fashion and deliberately avoids occasions which would call attention to those assumptions and make the reader's imagination balk. On a number of occasions Jarrell is not completely successful at this. When the gingerbread rabbit comes to live with the real rabbit couple, for example, this cookie engages in the incongruous act of munching on carrots and lettuce (Figure 7).

Such inconsistencies and incongruities are small things, but they make more difficult the reader's "willing suspension of disbelief" upon which the success of a fantasy rests. Without that good faith, a reader simply dismisses a work as unreal. This was the case of a student of mine who loved all of Jarrell's children's books except *The Gingerbread Rabbit*. Stumbling over the

42

Figure 7

few shortcomings in the fantasy, she finally seemed unwilling to suspend disbelief; reverting to a realistic criterion, she objected, "How can I take seriously the story of a mother who spends her day chasing through the woods after a cookie?" Such *realpolitik* and coolheaded pragmatism may seem out of place in the world of fantasy, but they reveal a shortcoming in *The Gingerbread Rabbit* which discouraged at least one otherwise sympathetic reader from entering into its world.

Another shortcoming to the book may be that the story leaves some matters unresolved. The role of Mary—the mother's child who leaves for school at the beginning of the story, the girl for whom the gingerbread rabbit is made, and the daughter who returns at the end of the day to find the sewn rabbit—remains unclear. In Jarrell's *Fly by Night* the link between the animal protagonist (the owl in "The Owl's Bedtime Story") and the child (David) is dramatically obvious and important. In *The Gingerbread Rabbit* any connection between the gingerbread rabbit and Mary is left unexplored.

The other matter that is left unresolved concerns the mother's motives. Williams clearly conveys this in one of his pictures (Figure 8). On the left is the distraught mother searching for the gingerbread rabbit as if she were searching for a lost child. On the right is the fearful rabbit trying to escape from the mother/giant who, he believes, wishes to eat him. Knowing this, a reader can only react to the picture with pathos. An unsettling tone of confusion seeps into the book. The story is full of regrettable misunderstandings and mistaken motives; and the gingerbread rabbit never, finally, learns what the mother's intentions were.

Much can be forgiven, however, since this was Jarrell's first children's book; he was still finding his way around an unfamiliar genre and would do better in his succeeding books. What *is* genuinely interesting is the way *The Gingerbread Rabbit* introduced themes Jarrell would use again with more skill in those other books.

As indicated, *The Gingerbread Rabbit* is a tale about mistaken motives and difficulties in communication. Similar misapprehensions and failures to communicate would appear in Jarrell's next book, *The Bat-Poet,* but they would serve a more definite purpose of portraying the difficulties of a poet in society.

Another theme lightly touched upon here, and more fully developed in the other books, is separation anxiety—a familiar childhood dilemma when two emotions compete: a worry about being separated from parents and the desire to become independent of them. This is, of course, a critical issue in the fairy tale behind *The Gingerbread Rabbit:* in the beginning, Hansel and Gretel are troubled when they are apart from their parents and desperately seek a way back to their house which they see as a sanctuary; later, the "house" (the gingerbread cottage) is seen as a prison and the parent (the witch) as someone difficult to escape from. Like the fairy tale, the book presents pairs of homes that offer security (the rabbits' cave, the squirrel's nest) or danger (the fox's cave, the mother's kitchen). And like the fairy tale, Jarrell's story deals with the twin emotions of separation anxiety: the mother's loving search through the woods for her lost creation can be seen as a projection of a child's wish to be found and not be apart from the parent; likewise, the gingerbread rabbit's anxiety about being caught by the mother is, like Hansel and Gretel's similar fear, an expression of the need to be independent.

"Chase me"—a game toddlers often play when they crawl away from their parents and then look over their shoulders to make sure they are being pursued—is an important part of childhood development. Like peek-a-boo or hide-and-seek, this game involves experiments in separateness. Significantly, then, when the mother is unable to provide her daughter with the

Figure 8

gingerbread rabbit, the fox suggests another kind of surprise: "Just stand behind the door and jump out and say *Boo!* at her when she comes in" (46). In a similar vein, the real rabbits make their offer of adoption more attractive to their gingerbread son by promising that he can "go out in the meadow and play hide-and-seek with us at night" (42). Aware of this theme, Williams's last illustration in the book presents the primordial image of the child's discovery of separateness: the artist pictures the gingerbread rabbit reaching for the moon (Figure 9).

While Jarrell only lightly touches upon the theme of separation anxiety in his first children's book, it would, in fact, become the central theme of his three subsequent books in the way his heroes leave and return or do not return to the original homes of their parents. Connected to this are two other important motifs which also were introduced in *The Gingerbread Rabbit*—the wish for companions and the theme of adoption.

The wish for companions has a conspicuous role. The gingerbread rabbit is not content to just run away from the kitchen; he spends his entire time in the woods searching for a needed friend and tries his luck with the squirrel and the fox until he comes to live with the real rabbits. On their part, the real rabbits so wanted "a little rabbit of [their] own," they had already prepared a bed of rushes for its arrival (42–43, Figure 10). Likewise, the extravagant behavior of Mary's mother—spending her day chasing a cookie through the woods, even offering the fox a position as the family pet—can only be understood if seen as a mother's earnest preoccupation with the idea of providing a companion for her daughter.

Mary Jarrell suggests possible biographical explanations behind the appearance of the theme of adoption when the elderly, childless couple of real rabbits take in their gingerbread son. After his parents separated and his mother and brother returned to Nashville, Jarrell spent a wonderful year living with

Figure 9

Figure 10

his grandparents in California. Like the gingerbread rabbit, only unsuccessfully, the eleven-year-old boy told the old couple, "I'd like to live with you always. Always!" (43). Seen in this fashion, *The Gingerbread Rabbit* may be wish-fulfillment: the boy living with the elderly couple; his mother and his sibling living some distance away in another house; and in his place, a sewn rabbit.

The wish for companions and for adoption play a notable part in Jarrell's subsequent children's books. The search for sympathetic friends is a motivating force for the bat-poet in Jarrell's next book. Later, in *Fly by Night,* a friendless boy named David is adopted by an owl and hears a bedtime story about a lonely owlet who acquires a companion. But these themes would be particularly important in *The Animal Family* where a lonely hunter acquires a companion in a mermaid and then adopts a bear, a lynx, and a boy. While not as accomplished as these later books, *The Gingerbread Rabbit* marked Jarrell's first foray into the world of children's books and introduced his themes.

Chapter Two

THE BAT-POET

W hat is striking about *The Bat-Poet,* Jarrell's second book
for children, is that it appeals to such diverse constitu-
encies. It seems a cult book among "struggling artists," like the
freelance photographer and reluctant owner of my local book-
store and the woman returning to school for creative writing
classes, both of whom have told me it is their favorite book.
Critics, too, prize the book, even consider it an important "alle-
gorical statement of modern poetics."[1] Literary gossips also like
the book, and when it first appeared (1964) saw it as a thinly
disguised portrait of Jarrell's feelings about such poets as Robert
Frost. Finally, it is a children's classic in classrooms across this
country where sixth-graders, enrolled in the Junior Great Books
Program, encounter *The Bat-Poet* between Jack London's "To
Build a Fire" and Lewis Carroll's *Alice's Adventures in Wonder-
land.*

Jarrell felt good about his story, which he described as
"half for children and half for grown-ups." In a radio interview
with Aaron Kramer, Jarrell said: "Sometimes you feel you have
good *luck* with a book. Things *come* to you. . . . You work on it

all the time. You stay awake at night, . . . wake up in the middle of the night."[2]

The day-dreaming reader can easily imagine Jarrell at home in Greensboro and unable to sleep as the story struggles within him. Staring out the window, he once again notes the bats hanging upside-down on his porch. *They* were sleeping. *He* was awake. He was different. Because, because, . . . because he was a poet. There was one bat different from the rest, a kind of *café-au-lait* brown. What if he was an insomniac? What if he was a poet?

Perhaps in a manner close to this, Jarrell came to write his story about a bat who is a poet. But why a bat and not, say, a Keatsian nightingale?

As Mary Jarrell has observed, one of her husband's most frequent literary devices is transposition; this explains, she suggests, something others find surprising in his poetry: among male poets, he is conspicuously different in often preferring female narrators.[3] Transposition (and its equivalent, the oxymoron) appear in various other ways in Jarrell's poetry. One only has to think of that poem anthologists seem to regard as *echte* Jarrell, "The Death of the Ball Turret Gunner." There is, first of all, the position of the gunner: he is hunched, like a bat, upside-down in his turret. Then there is the surprising revelation in the last line of the poem, that we are being told this story by a narrator who is already dead. Then, too, the oxymorons of the poem reverse conventional associations and portray death as a birth and a waking.

It should not be surprising, then, that Jarrell would choose so unconventional a creature as a bat as a figure for a poet; it is the only mammal that flies and an animal whose life is full of unusual transpositions—spending its days hanging upside-down and its nights awake. But Jarrell's choice also addresses

53

the regrettably common opinion that poets are "batty"—eccentric individuals with "bats in their belfry," odd and queer; in another fashion, he shows that the public is absolutely correct in their estimation—what is genuinely admirable about poets is how they are "different."

I

In her essay "The Group of Two," Mary Jarrell says something about the composition of her husband's second children's book and suggests how, after the fact, it can be read as a *roman à clef*: "In a hammock at one of his stations 'out in Nature' and with the FM on loud, Randall wrote his *Bat-Poet*. . . . In Life, Frost and Cal [Robert Lowell] were Mockingbirds; Michael di Capua and I were Chipmunks, of sorts; and Bob Watson and Randall were Bats."[4] *The Bat-Poet* is, as Mary Jarrell indicates, a book about a poet among poets and friends. It is also a discourse about the poet's role in a society that barely tolerates and largely ignores poetry—a subject Jarrell would address over and over again in the essays collected in *Poetry and the Age*. In a sense, this children's book is a modern version of "The Artist of the Beautiful" with the bat-poet playing the role of Hawthorne's aesthetic outsider, Owen Warland.[5]

From the first, the bat-poet has to adjust to being "different." He is not only a lighter color than the other bats, he also prefers to remain on the porch when the bat clan moves to the barn at the end of the summer; he urges them to return and when they decline, he is sad to have to forfeit their snuggling companionship. This loner is also different because he develops a bat version of insomnia: while his fellows sleep during the day, he remains awake and loves to listen to the mockingbird recite marvelous poems. When the little bat urges the other bats to also stay awake to listen to the poet, they once more decline his importuning. Finally, he is different, too, when he tries his hand (or wing) at poetry and attempts to recite to his fellow bats a poem about daytime—"At dawn, the sun shines like a million moons / And all the shadows are as bright as moonlight. . . ." (5)—but they interrupt and criticize him, so that he is hurt and silenced. "There was nobody for him to say the poems to," the narrator concludes (8).

Alienated from his community, the young bat suddenly has the idea that the mockingbird might listen to his poems; who might make a better listener, he seems to reason, than another poet (say, an avian version of Lowell or Frost)? Instead, the mockingbird is vain and peremptory and overbearing, and he assumes that everyone wants to listen to *his* poems and honors the bat with a recitation of his newest—"To a Mockingbird." When the timid bat begins to hesitatingly ask whether he might recite one of his own poems ("Do you suppose that I—that I could—"), the conceited mockingbird jumps into the gap ("That you could hear it again? Of course you can.") and vaingloriously repeats the performance a second and third time (10). At long last, the shy bat makes his request clear and—as the mockingbird adopts a studied pose of listening to a novice— the bat recites his poem about an owl.

When the mockingbird praises the poem in a technical way ("clever of you to have that last line two feet short"), the bat-poet is confused and the mockingbird explains: "The last line's iambic trimeter, . . . has six syllables and the one before it has ten" (14). Later, the bat-poet expresses irritation with such technical praise because it is beside the point: "What do I care how many feet it has? The owl nearly kills me, and he says he likes the rhyme-scheme!" Now it is the bat-poet who concludes, "The trouble isn't making poems, the trouble's finding somebody that will listen to them" (15).

While the association Mary Jarrell suggests between

Lowell and the mockingbird may be difficult to see, the resemblance between Frost and the mockingbird is unmistakable to those familiar with Frost's personality and idiosyncrasies. "To say a poem" was one of Frost's affectations that the mockingbird directly inherits, along with Frost's habit at poetry readings of adding, "I like having said that poem so much, let me say it again." Moreover, Frost's peremptory and authoritative way which abashed younger poets, his affectation of adopting a studied pose when listening, are also given to the bird.

But as unpleasant as many people found Frost personally, Jarrell would have been the first to acknowledge that he was, nonetheless, a great poet. In fact, Jarrell in essays almost singlehandedly championed Frost's poetry and brought the poet a measure of acceptability when his work was being overlooked by the then-reigning New Critics. But that was not all there was to their friendship. In a letter to Elizabeth Hardwick and Robert Lowell, Jarrell seems to describe his relationship to Frost as something like that of the bat-poet to the mockingbird, as the admiring listener: "I always treated him, when we talked, as Gorki did Tolstoy. . . . I asked and listened . . . (I *loved* to listen to him, really was fond of him). . . . I'm sure he couldn't make heads or tails out of anything else I wrote [besides my essays on him], and I'm sure he felt faintly, uncomfortably mocking about everything in me that hadn't written those articles; after all, nothing I did was the way *he'd* have done it."[6]

As Mary Jarrell suggests about this *roman à clef*, Jarrell found in his wife and his editor Michael di Capua the ideal listener; the bat-poet finds the same in the chipmunk. When the bat-poet recites to this equally timid creature the poem about the owl, the chipmunk responds appropriately—he shivers in fear. To honor him, bat-poet creates the chipmunk's "portrait in verse" ("The Chipmunk's Day") which pictures the animal streaking about, gathering nuts, and diving in his holes. Pleased, the chipmunk finally understands what a poem is: saying what something is "like" (25).

When the bat-poet discovers he cannot create a poem about everything (he is unable to do a verse portrait of the cardinal), it suddenly occurs to him to write about someone he knows well— the mockingbird. He creates a beautiful poem which, like the others, is quoted in its entirety in the book. The bat-poet seizes on what is unique about the bird: during the day this fiercely territorial creature drives everyone else out of the yard, but at night he creates perfect likenesses of the excluded (the songs of a thrush and thrasher and jay, the meowing of a cat):

> He imitates the world he drove away
> So well that for a minute, in the moonlight,
> Which one's the mockingbird? which one's the world?
>
> (28)

Is this backhanded compliment also a comment on Frost? In his interview with Aaron Kramer, Jarrell seems to struggle to amend this notion by suggesting that there is something of the mockingbird in every poet:

Jarrell: I've known a lot of artists and poets . . . and . . . I write poetry myself—or anyway, I write verse myself. . . . Several times when I've talked with writer friends about this book I'm amused to see how they immediately identify with the mockingbird. (Laugh) But the hero of the book is a bat who is really quite nice. And there's a charming chipmunk. And, well, the mockingbird is pretty bad. But he's a *real* artist. (Pause) Some of the time, as Keats says, "when a poet looks at sparrows playing in the gravel he *is* those sparrows" but the funny thing is . . . the rest of the time . . . most of the time, if he's a *normal* poet, he's just as vain as he can be and he's obsessed with *himself*. And mockingbirds are! Mockingbirds are the best birds in the world at imitating other birds. And everything else. They can imitate cars, distant trains, chipmunks. . . . But at the same time they imitate 'em, *perfectly,* get their real essence—*echte* chipmunk, and so on—they can't stand 'em. They drive 'em away. (Pause) . . . Territoriality at its strongest is in mockingbirds. . . . (Pause) So, it seemed to me that . . . mockingbirds are not only more like artists than other birds, they're more like people, too.

Kramer: Well, you're certainly not that kind of poet, Jarrell.

Jarrell: Oh . . . but . . . but if I'm not . . . I'm not a poet, I'm afraid. I mean . . . I mean . . . (Laugh).[7]

Much can be seen between the lines of Jarrell's comments. Certainly, the sensitivity to issues of status (writers of verse contrasted with real poets) is a sub-text which offers validity to the argument that poets (Jarrell included) are concerned with "territoriality." If the mockingbird is a figure for Frost, what can also be seen is the desire to mute or mitigate a genuine criticism of him ("pretty bad," "he's just as vain as he can be and he's obsessed with *himself*") through Jarrell's gambit of acknowledging the same faults in himself. Most important, however, is that in stressing the mockingbird's great gifts as a poet over his personal shortcomings, Jarrell wishes to make sure that he is not misunderstood as criticizing the bird or the poet.

The importance of this issue becomes clear when the bat-poet recites his poem about the mockingbird in the book. The chipmunk is impressed by the poem-portrait but warns, "He won't like it" (30). In fact, the mockingbird is irritated when he hears it: "You sound as if there were something wrong with imitating things! . . . with driving them off" (31). It is an awkward moment. The chipmunk tries to mollify the bird, the bat tries to explain that his motives have been mistaken, and the mockingbird complains that no one understands how "a mockingbird's *sensitive*" (32).

As if unsettled by his failure to communicate, by these crossed signals, the bat-poet begins to regress and "he began to think of the first things he could remember" (34). The result is a beautiful poem about a baby bat clinging to his mother and his mother folding her wings around him. The chipmunk—otherwise such a sympathetic listener but unable to understand why bats sleep by day, fly at night, see with their ears, and sleep upside down—finds the poem "really queer" (40).

As if unsettled by his favorite listener's response and the notion of how he is "different," the bat-poet decides that this is the poem which the other bats would understand, and he flies to the barn where they have begun their winter hibernation. Snuggling into their warm midst, he thinks to tell them the poem when they awake and recites it to himself, but starts to forget. He tries again, forgets, then thinks: "I wish I'd said we sleep all winter." The book ends with the bat-poet yawning into sleep, "snuggled closer to the others" (43).

In some ways, the conclusion is a disappointment. To be sure, and as Mary Jarrell suggests, this might be viewed as a "happy ending": the bat-poet *has* written a poem about bats, and perhaps (as the chipmunk suggests) the other bats, the sleeping masses, are sure to like it when they wake. Still, in the comfort of snuggling companionship, poetry is forgotten.

The conclusion is disappointing because what is admirable about the little bat is his choice to be a poet at the risk of being different, and his success is measured by the distance he puts between himself and the other bats; it seems unfortunate, then, though understandable, that he returns to them in the end— even more so when, having expressed a decided preference for the porch, he goes at last to the barn. He goes there, of course, for the best reasons—to recite his poetry—however, his trip does not seem to be occasioned by a new self-confidence, but by a feeling of being wounded by his friend, the chipmunk, who thinks his poem "queer." Likewise, the bat-poet's assertion of his individuality is symbolized in the story by his remaining awake while others sleep and by his attentiveness to poetry; it is disappointing, consequently, that the story should end with his falling asleep amidst those most indifferent to poetry. Finally, it is sad that, having worked so hard on his poem about bats, the bat-poet begins to forget it and falls asleep before he has the occasion to recite it. These observations may seem unfair since he is, after all, a bat and it is quite natural that he would hibernate; still, this seasonal choice falls within Jarrell's artistic prerogatives.

In a fashion, the conclusion of *The Bat-Poet* gives expression to a frequent wish Jarrell would articulate in such essays as "The Obscurity of the Poet"—the wish that poets would be accepted by a society largely indifferent to them. In a memorial lecture at the Library of Congress after Jarrell's death, Karl Shapiro identified the conditions that gave rise to this wish:

> Jarrell's generation inherited the question of Culture—
> Mass Culture versus True Culture. . . . Jarrell said the
> acceptably righteous things about Mass Culture, that mass
> culture either corrupts or isolates the writer, that "true
> works of art are more and more produced away from or in
> opposition to society." And yet he knew the writer's need
> for contact with the mass and qualified his rejections of the
> Medium. Part of the artist, he said (I am quoting now from
> *A Sad Heart at the Supermarket*), "wants to be like his kind;
> longs to be loved and admired and successful."

Shapiro summarized the dilemma in this fashion: "Whether to be a bat or a poet: that is the question."[8]

If *The Bat-Poet* ends happily, it does so by conveying the

hope that someday in the future, society—now all wrapped up in itself like hibernating bats—may give the poets and artists the attention they deserve. If the book ends tragically, it is because, in the meantime, individuals who long for snuggling companionship can only join the somnolent flock by forgetting they are poets and artists.

II

But *The Bat-Poet* was not just for grown-ups; it was also "half for children." This notion of a double audience tickled Jarrell; in his radio interview with Aaron Kramer he mentioned that the *New Yorker* had printed two of the poems that later appeared in the book: "I didn't tell them they were children's poems. (Laugh) It was probably a great shock for them to find that out later."[9]

What is there for children in the book? What is it that would lead to its inclusion by educators among the readings for sixth-graders involved in the Great Books program? And what accounts for its popularity among child readers unconcerned about the rivalries between poets or the issue of the artist's role in society?

Peter Neumeyer and Perry Nodelman have suggested reasons why the book is or should be popular with educators.[10] It explains what a poet is and, accurately, how he or she works. It also answers a fundamental question raised by children: Just what is a poem—that thing which appears so typographically different on a page, that thing with its frequent rhythms and occasional rhymes? In this sense *The Bat-Poet* is a kind of primer that can be used to introduce poetry—which is (the chipmunk points out) saying what something is "like," which is (to quote W. H. Auden) "memorable speech."

These lessons do explain why *The Bat-Poet* would be popular with educators putting together their booklists. But if instruction were all there was to the book, it might have little appeal to children. Trying to account for the popularity of her classic *Mary Poppins* books, P. L. Travers explained to me that: "All school teaching is a direct giving of information. But everything I do . . . [is indirect and] gets into the inner ear. . . . I suppose if there is something in my books that appeals to children, it is the result of my not having to go *back* to my childhood; I can, as it were, turn *aside* and consult it."[11]

Randall Jarrell was also gifted in this way. His children's books were written at the same time he was composing the autobiographical poems of *The Lost World* which recounted his own childhood. But even so, in all of his poems, Karl Shapiro has argued, the child is the center of value. Where other poets might turn for their roots to mythology or belief, Jarrell, because of his interest in psychoanalysis, turned to "the First Impression, the earliest consciousness. . . . Jarrell was the poet of the *Kinder* and the earliest games of the mind and heart."[12]

Childhood memories, the First Impression, the earliest consciousness, were sources of inspiration for Jarrell, as they are for his bat-poet; in fact, the idea for the poem the little bat is most satisfied with (his poem about bats) began in a sort of waking dream: "For some reason, he began to think of the first things he could remember." In a similar fashion, *The Bat-Poet* itself seems in part inspired by what Jarrell called "a recurrent scene from my childhood." Jarrell's mother suffered from a mysterious disorder that caused her to faint, and in the poem "Hope" Jarrell describes how he and his brother felt when this occurred:

It was as if God were taking a nap.

We waited for the world to be the world
And looked out, shyly, into the little lanes

That went off from the great dark highway, Mother's
  Highway
And wondered whether we would ever take them—

And she came to life, and we never took them.[13]

This timidity, this uncertainty, this shyness also charac-
terizes the bat-poet. Independence *is* an unsettling affair, when
all the other bats drift off to sleep and he remains awake, when
all the other bats go to the barn and he remains on the porch.
But what is different is that the bat-poet (unlike the child in the
poem) *does* take those highways, *does* leave the warm and snuggling and sleeping world of maternal security behind and strike
out on his own.

This exploration makes *The Bat-Poet* appealing to children
and speaks to their "inner ear." By being able to turn aside and
consult his own childhood apprehensions, Jarrell was able to
draw a portrait of something all children face: the uneasiness
that comes with striking out on one's own, the courage and per-
ils associated with being "different," the need to "cut the apron
strings" and leave the nest, the wish for approval and fears of
rejection. These are all so much a part of childhood, from the
day one crosses the street by one's self to the day one leaves
home and goes to school. Jarrell did not forget his childhood,
and children prize his book for that.

III

After he had sent his story to his publisher, Jarrell was at first
surprised and unnerved when he learned that his editor had
assigned the task of illustrating the book to Maurice Sendak, an
artist whose talents were just then beginning to be recognized.
He presumed that, having illustrated *The Gingerbread Rabbit*,
Garth Williams would continue as his illustrator. But when the

pictures meant to accompany the book were finally shown to him, Jarrell concluded di Capua had made the right decision.

He was keen about everything Sendak had done, from the choices of paper and printing to the drawings which captured the "lyrical" quality of the story and were elevated in a "classical" way so the book would appeal to both adults and children. Jarrell went on to tell di Capua: "I'm crazy about the small bat drawings at the side (of the pages), the ones he [Sendak] added at the last."[14]

My own enthusiasm for Sendak's pictures does not extend to these marginal bats. To be sure, thematic justifications can be offered for all those bats tucked into the corners of pages—they say something about a creature who prefers the corners of the world, and their position on the page coincides with Jarrell's point that artists are "marginal" people in society. Still, they seem like an afterthought, like doodles on the manuscript, and make the pages too "busy."

Looking back at the book ten years later, Sendak told me that he believes *The Bat-Poet* is "the best constructed and artistically controlled" of Jarrell's stories, but that he himself was happier with the pictures he had done for Jarrell's *Fly by Night*. As good as they are, the shortcomings of *The Bat-Poet*'s pictures seem due to Sendak's not having completely settled on a style, as he has in his other masterpieces. On the one hand, some of his pictures recall the personable accuracy of Beatrix Potter's miniatures of animal life; indeed, Jarrell would observe that "some of them are the most accomplished drawings of bats I've ever seen."[15] On the other hand, the pictures shift from miniatures to the panoramic perspective of landscape painting and seem, unlike his "decorations" for *The Animal Family*, vestigial stage settings. Finally, the brilliant "conversation" between picture and text, present in *Fly by Night,* is missing here.[16]

Sendak's genius shines through, however, in some pictures which do not simply illustrate but also interpret the story. In one, for example, Sendak portrays the owl and (in the lower right corner) a mouse timidly hiding at the base of a tree (Figure 11). In another, Sendak shows the territorial mockingbird holding forth while an abashed cat cowers at the base of a tree (Figure 12). The compositions are so similar that Sendak invites a comparison and a conclusion: the owl and the mockingbird are alike; both are intimidating creatures.

Jarrell and Sendak felt that a kind of sympathetic collaboration, at a deep psychic or unconscious level, had occurred in the book. Mary Jarrell mentioned that when she and her husband first saw Sendak's pictures they were struck by how the artist, never having visited their home, had uncannily reproduced the exact corner of their house where the bats clustered and had likewise (by "some inexplicable empathy") drawn an incredible likeness to their garden right down to its wooden bench.

Sendak said something similar in a conversation with Selma Lanes:

> When the pictures for *The Bat-Poet* were finished, it was remarkable, because as Jarrell and I looked over the illustrations together, there were images in the art which he had never discussed with me; images which appeared as though we had picked each other's brains. There was, for example, a drawing of a lion at the end of the book, though no lion is mentioned in the poem at all. Jarrell was greatly startled; not only was the lion his special favorite beast, it had been that image that evoked the poem originally. He hadn't transmitted this fact to me in any way, yet the lion was there. To me, this was one of those unique moments of collaboration. [17]

Sendak admits that he often "lets himself go" on a wordless

Figure 11

Figure 12

double-page spread, a conspicuous feature in all his master-pieces (e.g., *Where the Wild Things Are, In the Night Kitchen, Outside Over There*). These are "dream visions," he has explained, where his unconscious connects to the story in personal and idiosyncratic ways. And Sendak's lion (which had not been mentioned in Jarrell's story) appears on just such a double-page spread in *The Bat-Poet* (Figure 13).

Something else is remarkable about this picture. In a fashion, it establishes a link between the bat-mother and the owl because it echoes a smaller double-page spread earlier in the book (Figure 14). Both picture moonlit nights, both portray mothers and children at the base of trees (the lioness and her cub, the opossum and her babies), but the owl of the earlier spread takes the place of the bat-mother. Sendak made the same statement twelve years later in the wordless double-page spread of *Fly by Night* by making it an echo of its counterparts in *The Bat-Poet*: again a moonlit night, again mothers and children at the base of trees (mother and infant, ewe and lambs), and again prominence given to an aerial creature—but instead of the bat-mother in the upper-right corner of the wordless double-page spread, in *Fly by Night* Sendak pictures the owl.

Sendak's pictures, in other words, direct attention to the owl, a creature who might otherwise seem a minor character in the book. And by suggesting a link between the owl and the bat-mother, Sendak intimates something which can make visible the resemblances between *The Bat-Poet* and *The Gingerbread Rabbit*.

The owl is the most threatening creature in the book: the chipmunk hides from it; the bat-poet fears it; and the poem about the owl addresses this. In contrast, the least threatening and most loving creature in the book is the bat-mother; and the poem about her addresses this. What is remarkable is that, despite their differences, the poems about the owl and the bat-mother are, in a sense, homologous. The owl is "a shadow float-ing in the moonlight," while "in the moonlight" the bat-mother and her child make "a single shadow, printed on the moon." Both the owl and the bat-mother are explorers of the night:

> [The owl's] eyes try all the corners of the night.

> It calls and calls: all the air swells and heaves
> And washes up and down like water.
>
> (12)

> [The bat-mother's] high sharp cries
> Like shining needlepoints of sound
> Go out into the night and, echoing back,
> Tell her what they have touched.
>
> (36)

But the differences in this analogy are significant; the owl is threatening and makes timid creatures fearful for their lives—

> The ear that listens to the owl believes
> In death. The bat beneath the eaves,

> The mouse beside the stone are still as death—
> The owl's air washes them like water.
> The owl goes back and forth inside the night,
> And the night holds its breath.
>
> (12)

—but the poem about the bat-mother emphasizes the help-lessness of her baby ("A bat is born / Naked and blind . . .") and the security the mother provides as she "flaps home to her rafter" and "folds her wings about her sleeping child" (36–37).

These similarities suggest the reappearance of the mother who is both threatening and loving. She is *The Gingerbread Rab-bit*'s fox and rabbit-mother, *The Bat-Poet*'s owl and bat-mother.

Figure 13

Figure 14

This figure in the background makes the gingerbread rabbit's and the bat-poet's forays into independence so unsettling; she also makes them so eager to find a snug hole and a warm home. Jarrell seems only dimly aware of this element in these stories, but in the book which followed *The Bat-Poet* he would deal with it consciously.

Chapter Three

FLY BY NIGHT

I n the realm of illustrated children's books, *Fly by Night* exists on some high haunted aerie. It is a paramount example of the synthesis of text and illustration, each amplifying and enriching the other. And it shows two artists at their best: Jarrell's story is among his most profound; Sendak's pictures, among his strongest.

Jarrell and Sendak had collaborated before. Still, *Fly by Night* was special—as Sendak indicated when I asked him which was his favorite: "Of the three, my personal favorite is *The Animal Family*. I think the best constructed and artistically controlled is *The Bat-Poet*. But, in terms of the pictures, my favorite is *Fly by Night*."

Jarrell sensed this and, in the midst of writing, sent Sendak a letter: "This new book—it's a sort of dream book, all in the present tense—is named *Fly by Night*. . . . [It] will be so easy for you to illustrate that I've laughed over the thought again and again. . . . Paragraph by paragraph it divides into pictures, and pictures thoroughly in your own style."[1]

Jarrell was wrong; it was not easy for Sendak to do the illustrations. A few months after this letter, Jarrell was struck by a car and killed. Saddened by the loss of his friend, Sendak was unable to start work on the story for ten years.

As a consequence, *Fly by Night,* Jarrell's third children's book, was not published until 1976; *The Animal Family,* his fourth children's book, appeared before it did. In conversation, Sendak explained his responsibility for this decade-long delay:

> I read the story and thought it was the most difficult one of all of them. We had only a brief time together because he was killed not long after [in 1965]. Then it was ten years from that time before I felt I could do it. I kept postponing it over and over again because I felt very complicated about the story and because I missed him so much I didn't want to do it. When a decade had passed, I felt far enough away from his death to try it again. *Fly by Night*'s pictures were really worth waiting ten years for. I couldn't do *Fly by Night* until I had done *The Juniper Tree.* [Published in 1973, *The Juniper Tree and Other Tales from Grimm* was Sendak's watershed book. He provided intense, Dürer-like illustrations for twenty-seven Grimm fairy tales, four of which had been translated by Jarrell and the remainder by Lore Segal.] That was the breakthrough for me in how to interpret Jarrell. I had to struggle so much with the Grimm, and I felt I had succeeded. I felt brave enough to try *Fly by Night* then, and it sort of fell into place. And I know he would have liked what I'd done. Still, it was a consolation to hear from Mary after the book was published that "Randall would have loved this." I felt good about that.

Fly by Night is a haunting book with pictures that invite brooding. Accustomed to cheerier children's books, I have heard parents wonder whether this book might not be too spooky and unnerving for children. John Updike, for example, made this point when he reviewed the book for the *New York Times* and said it has a "true forlornness" absent from such childhood classics as "Cinderella" or E. B. White's *Charlotte's Web*.[2] What parents forget is that children often have stronger stomachs than adults and that the childhood attraction to fairy tales reveals their appetite for grim truths; what Updike forgot is that White's book ends with Charlotte's death and that many of the great children's classics (*The Adventures of Huckleberry Finn*, for example) are truly forlorn. Personally, I have yet to encounter or hear of a child who has not liked *Fly by Night*.

I

The aerial and nocturnal interests of *The Bat-Poet* were continued in *Fly by Night*, but the plot and themes had been anticipated in both of Jarrell's two previous children's books. In the earlier books the action revolves around a character who leaves one world, passes through an interlude of independence in a new world that is sometimes dangerous, and finally reaches security in the end. Both books are marked by the hero's strong wish for companions and ambivalent feelings toward figures for a mother who is both loving and threatening. *Fly by Night* is about a boy and an owl-mother, follows a similar plot line, and reveals the intimate connection between the wish for companions and ambivalent feelings toward a mother.

Fly by Night is the story of a shy and lonely boy named David. He lives in the country and, because "there aren't any children for him to play with," he spends his waking hours daydreaming in his tree house. His only friends there are the swallows, but when he climbs the tree with his cat the birds grow uneasy and fly away. Even the cat "never stays long" (4).

That is how David spends his days. At night he exercises an angelic prerogative: "At night David can fly. In the daytime he can't. In the daytime he doesn't even remember that he can" (4–5).

But David is not only gifted with aerial mobility ("It isn't flying exactly, but floating"), he is also clairvoyant and can see others' dreams (5). When he floats into his parents' bedroom he sees his father's dream of carrying David on his back, his mother's dream mixed with pancakes and feathers. When he floats outdoors he sees his dog's dream of chasing a rabbit, his cat's dream of chasing mice.

The cat tells David that the mice in its dream are "dancing." But as Sendak's picture makes clear, the mice are not dancing; they're afraid for their lives and hide near the base of the tree as the striped cat malevolently eyes them. In this scene, Sendak pictures David curled in a fetal position, sleeping in this tree—David's safe place, his womb (Figure 15).

When David sees the mice aren't "dancing," he wants to tell the cat, "They're afraid of you" (10), but for some reason he can't. When he wants to stroke the cat, he is unable to move his arm, just as when he wants to say, "Wait! Wait!" to a fleeing rabbit, "he can't" (13). He is strangely impotent, as powerless as Huckleberry Finn, another floater, when in his tree perch he cannot save his friend Buck Grangerford.

This impotence reveals something of David's loneliness and crippling shyness. His inability to befriend others is also shown in subsequent incidents—when he passes over the rabbit, it flees; when he floats over the sheep, they're all asleep; when he wants to pet one of the ponies, they all shy and run to the barn. He is a floater, not a dynamically aerial Superman, and all his potential companions are the Clark Kents of the animal world— timid mice, skittery rabbit, sheepish sheep, shy ponies—who take flight at his appearance.

In this way, *Fly by Night* addresses the wish for companions evident in Jarrell's two previous children's books. Like the gingerbread rabbit, David seeks friends in a threatening world

Figure 15

of pursuers and the chase. Like the bat-poet, he is estranged and has difficulty communicating.

Help finally comes to this shy and lonely boy in the form of a night bird awake like himself. David is befriended by a striped owl with haunting eyes and a fish in its claws. This last item surprises David: "I didn't know owls could catch *fish*" (17). This discovery, that owls are predators, is a small matter but a significant one; it resembles Jarrell's childhood surprise at seeing "Mama" (his grandmother) wring a chicken's neck. And Sendak intimates its importance by picturing a fish on the back of the book's dustjacket.

The owl then speaks to David in poetry and invites him to her nest:

> My nest is in the hollow tree,
> My hungry nestlings wait for me.
> I've fished all night along the lake,
> And all for my white nestlings' sake.
> Come, little nestling, you shall be
> An owl till morning—you shall see
> The owl's white world, till you awake
> All warm in your warm bed, at daybreak.
>
> (18)

Through the night, the owl's nest serves as a warm place of parental security in a threatening world. This is, of course, the same place where David spends his days and the hollow tree where the frightened mice hide from the cat. It is also like the cozy hole where the gingerbread rabbit escapes from his pursuers and finds a bed and parents waiting for him, and like the barn where the bat-poet retreats from his disappointments and snuggles amidst his hibernating kin.

There David finds two waiting owlets. To hard-nosed David, they look sad and absurd in their unfeathered state, but he can see in the loving eyes of their mother that she "doesn't know the way they look" (19). David accepts the owl's invitation to be a "little nestling" until morning, and during the remainder of the night is treated as the gingerbread rabbit is treated by the real rabbits once he reaches their snug and safe home—as an adopted son.

Since daybreak is approaching, the owl-mother tells her three nestlings "The Owl's Bedtime Story," a long poem inserted into the text and the key to *Fly by Night*. It is the story of an owlet who wishes for companions. A great owl comes to this lonely owlet and tells him his wish can only be fulfilled if he leaves the security of his mother's nest:

> You shall have a sister of your own,
> A friend to play with, if, now, you will fly
> From your dark nest into the harsh unknown
> World the sun lights.
>
> (21)

The owlet departs, struggles through the tumult of "unfriendly day," and finally meets and befriends a sisterly companion, another owlet in a tree at whose base a dead owl lies. The two of them wend their way back through the harsh sunlight and the threatening crows until they arrive at the original nest where they welcome the arrival of the moon and the return of the owl both call "Mother." Like the bat-mother in Jarrell's previous book, she brings them food and folds her wings about them.

Once the owl has told this bedtime story, she accompanies David home. He wakes from his dream to sunlight and, like the bat-poet, starts slowly to forget. As David's mother calls him and begins to prepare pancakes, he struggles twice to remember, to link night and day in a simile: "the owl looks at me like—," his mother "looks at him like—" but before he can remember, sunlight streams into the kitchen and "his mother looks at him like his mother" (29–30).

II

Fly by Night would not be the same book without Sendak's pictures; these are not the gratuitous additions of an illustrator but something that furthers and amplifies the story. Here author and artist function as equals, and Sendak confessed to me his opinion that "*Fly by Night* is my book as much as it is Randall's."

Where David lacks the power of "like," Sendak is gifted. When the book ends, for example, we might expect an illustrator to provide a picture of David's mother in the kitchen preparing him pancakes. Instead, Sendak gives us her likeness: the cat on the kitchen table and, in the window behind her, a fledgling swallow struggling to fly by day (Figure 16).

It is an extraordinarily dense picture. The fledgling swallow is seen through three screening devices: a closed window, a half-open shade, and pulled curtains. These seem to serve the same purpose as the German shepherd Sendak introduced and positioned between the children and the witch in his illustration for "Hansel and Gretel" in *The Juniper Tree;* conceding that the dog does not appear in the Grimm's tale, Sendak explained, "I got her into the act to guard the children."[3] As the screening devices suggest, he felt a similar need to protect the fledgling from threat of the cat. Just what that threat might be is intimated by the locale: the feline has taken a dominant place in the kitchen.

Facing directly forward, this cat is clearly the same brooding creature who eyed the "dancing mice." Moreover, the cat's eyes and stripes recall those of the owl in the double-page spread—the owl, David noted, who held a small fish in her claws. Finally, the position of the cat on the left side of the picture mirrors the frontispiece where Sendak portrays David's dog in the lower right corner (Figure 17).

This picture is also multi-leveled. In the foreground is the

Figure 16

Figure 17

dog whose eyes recall those of the cat and the owl, and who (like them) faces forward. Behind the dog is the same fledgling swallow struggling to fly. And behind the bird is another vulnerable flier—David in his tree, outside his tree house. Behind that is another house, David's home, the original owl's nest.

Sendak's pictures, in other words, do not simply illustrate the story but go on to a deeper level to interpret it. What they suggest is what Jarrell said—in a completely different context—about his poem "A Quilt Pattern": "The child dreams of everything in terms of himself and his mother. There is nobody else in the dream."[4] There is nobody else in *Fly by Night*, David's dream. David's mother is the owl, the cat, the dog. And David is the owlet, swallow, mice, squirrel, rabbit, ponies, fish.

Throughout these pictures Sendak illuminates "the owl's white world" with the same power he brought to the Grimm's in *The Juniper Tree*. In Jarrell's previous book, the bat-poet tried to tell the other bats what the world looked like in the daylight: "the sun shines like a million moons / And all the shadows are as bright as moonlight" (5). In the nocturnal and moonlit world of *Fly by Night* things are also reversed and oddly different, "nothing is it own color": "the garden is striped black and white," the forest has "white limbs and black shadows," and "the white moon makes the black sky gray" (13, 17). In his cross-hatchings, in his blacks and whites, Sendak embodies Jarrell's nocturnal hallucinations and recreates the lunar brilliance of the story.

Sendak's David is naked as he floats by the light of the moon, a fact that disturbed John Updike when he reviewed the book.[5] He is naked, Sendak explained to me,

> because he is dreaming. Because between him and the dream there can be no clothing. It's a most personal thing for him. You don't want him dressed when something that personal is happening. My conception of personal experi-

85

ence as exposure—of your soul, but also literally of your body—really stems from my love for William Blake and *Songs of Innocence and Experience* where people are naked. They're not naked to titillate people; they're naked because they're yielding up their most personal moment when they give themselves up to their dream or their fantasy or their wish. To have David in pj's or Fruit-of-the-Loom shorts while he's having this . . . it would have been horrible. He had to be only David.

That reasoning would have been understood by Jarrell, who wrote: "Aren't works of art in some sense a way of doing without clothes, a means by which a reader, writer, and subject are able once to accept their own nakedness? the nakedness not merely of the 'naked truth,' but also of the naked wishes that come before and after that truth?"[6]

In his own work, in the first book of his trilogy (*Where the Wild Things Are*), Sendak tells the story of Max who (like Jarrell's David) departs his home, goes on a dream journey, and returns. In the second book (*In the Night Kitchen*), Mickey goes on a similar journey but this time the hero is a naked boy who flies. And the third book (*Outside Over There*), published after *Fly by Night,* features Ida, another aerial child who floats over her world and also goes on a dream journey. I asked Sendak if these shared themes explained why he felt close to Jarrell's book and why he felt so good about the way his own pictures worked together with Jarrell's text. He suggested there was also something more:

> I felt I joined him in spirit in this book. In so many of Randall's things, including *The Animal Family* and much of the poetry, there is a painful longing for a mother. *Fly by Night* is like an open declaration of the need for a mother— the whole poem about the owl and the babies, David being alone and coming back to his mother in the end. I had lost

my mother just a few years before the Jarrell book, and I had difficulties with my mother. This book was a way of resolving many personal issues via his issues. It was Mother we were both talking about in that particular book. And I was able to talk about my mother through his mother; I was also able to substitute my mother for his mother. Pictorially, my mother is in the book all the time. She is on the cover of the book; that's taken from a photograph of my mother in her wedding gown [Figure 18]. In the double-page spread that's my mother on the far right as a young girl in Europe, a shepherdess; in the middle, that's my mother holding me under a tree. She's overweight having borne three children; and on either side are two lambs—one is my brother and one is my sister [Figure 19]. The book was an *hommage* to my mother.

The double-page spread in *Fly by Night* is an example of the artist's lunar brilliance. Sendak went on to explain: in the scene David floats against the mammoth and brooding eyes of the owl ("the owl is a threatening bird but also a loving bird; and what I think I'm saying is that's what mothers are"), above paired ducks and rabbits ("because he didn't have a pair of parents, I gave Randall one in this vision"), above a fox ("which could have come from *The Gingerbread Rabbit,* I'm not sure"), above a shepherdess and her flock ("counting sheep, that's the way some people fall asleep"), and above a mother and child near whom is a small plank carved with the name "Angelina."

III

David lives in the same mythopoeic world where angels are made. It is the world of the child and the primitive where "like" has no force and invisible passions and emotions must be wholly made over into physical and concrete things—angels, gods, wise

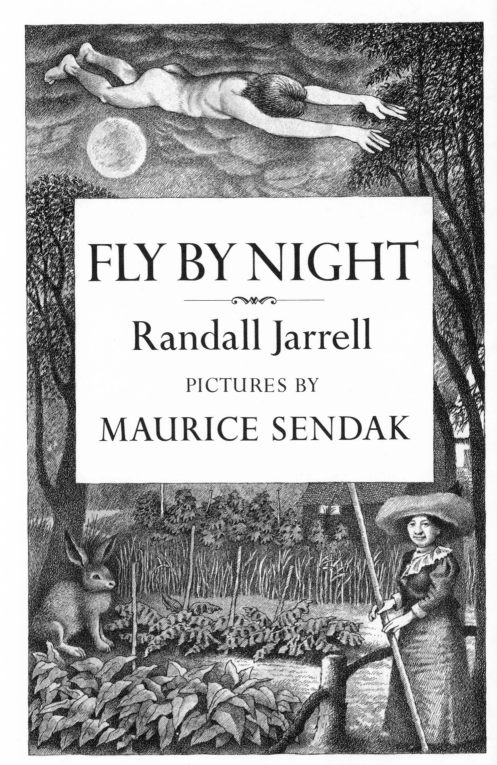

FLY BY NIGHT

Randall Jarrell

PICTURES BY

MAURICE SENDAK

Figure 18

owls. It is not a world of linking similes; David, in the end, cannot say how the owl is "like" his mother. Instead, it is a world of strict separations of night from day, child from companions, mother from child that become other separations: "dancing mice" and frightened mice, unfeathered owlets and lovable offspring, hard-nosed literality and what is figured in dreams.

David has, in other words, no notion of psychology. At the moment he comes closest to this, he stops short: David thinks the owl speaks "in such a low deep voice it is almost like hearing it inside his head" (18). At his age, David is pre-analytical. There is much in *Fly by Night*, Mary Jarrell observes, "for the Freudian initiate . . . [but] David knows none of this." Children *have* dreams; it is adults who interpret them.

Jarrell was comfortable with Freudian interpretation. If he hadn't become a teacher, his wife has said, he would have been content to have become a psychoanalyst; what prevented him from doing so was the "blood"—the requirement in this country that psychoanalysts first acquire the M.D. A picture of Freud always graced their living room, and when Jarrell started sporting a beard he fancied a resemblance between himself and the Austrian thinker. Freud's works always appeared on the booklists for the classes Jarrell taught, and psychoanalysts occasionally show up in his poems. [7]

In Freudian terms, then, what is *Fly by Night*, David's dream, all about? As "The Owl's Bedtime Story" makes clear, the book deals with separation anxiety and its resolution. David feels a strong bond of affection for his mother, but that bond also constitutes a threat: if he wants to gain companions, he must break that bond, cut the apron strings, leave the nest.

David's affectionate bond arises from the Oedipus Complex. This becomes clear when he floats over his parents and sees "their" dreams. The boy's oedipal wish to displace his fa-

Figure 19

ther appears when David sees a dream of himself on his father's shoulders, and while his father looks very small, David "is as big as ever" (6). The boy's oedipal desire to be the sole object of his mother's attention is evident in the dream he sees of his mother making pancakes, a dream all mixed up with the feathers of her pillow. The feathers, of course, prepare for the mother's transformation into the owl; the pancakes—those gifts of food and affection which become the food the nurturing owl-mother provides for her nestlings—reappear when David's mother cooks them for him, alone, in the book's conclusion.

As the story progresses, David's dilemma is articulated in "The Owl's Bedtime Story":

> There was once upon a time a little owl.
> He lived with his mother in a hollow tree.
> On winter nights he'd hear the foxes howl,
> He'd hear his mother call, and he would see
> The moonlight glittering upon the snow.
> How many times he wished for company
> As he sat there alone! He'd stand on tiptoe,
> Staring across the forest for his mother,
> And hear her far away; he'd look below
> And see the rabbits playing with each other
> And see the ducks together on the lake
> And wish that he'd a sister or a brother.
> Sometimes it seemed to him his heart would break.
> The hours went by, slow, dreary, wearisome,
> And he would watch, and sleep a while, and wake—
> "Come home! Come home!" he'd think; and she would come
> At last, and bring him food, and they would sleep.
>
> (20–21)

"The Owl's Bedtime Story" sounds two themes simultaneously. On the one hand (and in a distinct echo of the poem about the bat-mother in Jarrell's previous book), the owlet in its nest desperately misses its mother, doesn't want to be parted from her, and is relieved when she returns and folds her wings around him. On the other hand, the owlet longs for companions: "How many times he wished for company . . . that he'd a sister or a brother."

The connection between these two themes becomes evident as "The Owl's Bedtime Story" continues and the great owl tells the owlet, "you shall have a sister of your own, / A friend to play with, if, now, you will fly / From your dark nest." The owlet does take that risk and, as the great owl promised, he finds another owlet, a sisterly companion, in a distant tree.

In this way, Jarrell returns to his perennial theme—separation anxiety and its resolution. Separation anxiety is pictured in the desperation the owlet feels in the absence of his mother. To speak of its resolution, Jarrell has created the story equivalent of "leaving the nest"; the resolution of separation anxiety comes when a child is willing to forfeit its dependence on its mother, "cut the apron strings," "leave the nest." (In the Grimm's "Hansel and Gretel," this resolution is symbolized in a different manner in the tale's symbolic matricide, and there is a hint of this in "The Owl's Bedtime Story" when the owlet befriends the orphan owlet who rests in the distant tree at the base of which lies a dead owl.) The wish for companions, in other words, is intimately connected to and frustrated by separation anxiety; friends can only be won by separating from the mother.

"The Owl's Bedtime Story" is the key to *Fly by Night* and pictures David's problem and its solution. It also explains why a Freudian interpretation reveals so many ambivalent mother figures in the other parts of David's dream. Like the owlet, David loves his mother but needs to fly from her, misses his mother but needs to escape from her. And so, by projection, she seems to him both loving and threatening—a version of *The Gingerbread Rabbit*'s rabbit-mother and fox, *The Bat-Poet*'s bat-mother and owl, *The Lost World*'s Mama who is also a Judith holding a chicken whose neck she has wrung. She is the loving owl-mother of *Fly by Night* who also has a fish in her claws, the affectionate pets (the cat and the dog) who also pursue rabbits and squirrels or make mice and swallows feel uneasy. And David is an owlet, a swallow, a mouse, a squirrel, a rabbit, a fish.

In "The Owl's Bedtime Story" the owlet *does* heroically leave the nest and *does* make a friend. It is a step forward into maturity: as the two owlets fly together, they "feel so satisfied, / So grown-up!" (23). They return to the original nest and the owl both call "Mother," who wraps her wings around them. The lonely owlet gets both his wishes—mother love and a friend.

In this way, *Fly by Night* approaches a more fully resolved conclusion than does *The Bat-Poet*, despite their apparent similarities. While the return of the bat-poet to his hibernating (and undifferentiated) kin may seem a disappointment after his heroic interlude of independence, the return of the owlets to Mother is completely understandable in terms of their age. These are not the mature birds of Whitman's "Out of the Cradle Endlessly Rocking" who are a romantic couple; they are too young to make a nest of their own, and the owlet thinks of his companion as a sister-friend, not as a wife. This home-away-home structure is entirely appropriate and traditional in a fantasy about pre-adolescence.

The conclusion of *Fly by Night* also intimates a salutary resolution of David's problems, despite the fact that he is unable to say how the owl is "like" his own mother. At his age, we would not expect him to interpret his dream. Instead, it is enough that he stands on the brink of linking simile, that he "knows" the dream answer to his problem in a child's pre-analytical manner, at an unconscious level. In *Fly by Night* Jarrell,

the adult, seems to treat more consciously the relationship between mother and child which had otherwise been a latent subject in his two previous children's books.

Fly by Night is just the book for children at David's age,
poised at the onset of puberty—all those daydreaming youths
seen on a walk through a junior-high school, their heads on
their desks drawing pictures of what?—airplanes, sailboats. *Fly
by Night* is read and will be read by dreamy youths like David,
those same kids who in their tree houses read of others who
were ordinary but—like Tarzan or Superman or Peter Pan—
have a double life and are aerial, too. It is a kind of gift by Jarrell
(the author of *The Bat-Poet*) and Sendak (the artist of *In the
Night Kitchen*) to youths in love with night and the creatures
that—like Batman or Dracula or Zorro—are vivid then but
grow anemic at daybreak.

But *Fly by Night* also speaks directly to adults—to men
nestled in their easy chairs with books that transport them to
the knightly world of detectives. It speaks to women, curled up
like David in his tree, their knees under their chin, who have
gone with the wind and dream of moonlight trysts on mansion
savannahs. *Fly by Night* is for us, Davids, hard-nosed and slow
to "like," for whom fantasy provides what we cannot find at
daybreak: a way to be in dreams awake.

Chapter Four

THE ANIMAL FAMILY

Little of what is remarkable in Jarrell's *The Animal Family* is evident, P. L. Travers has observed, in the simplicity of its plot.[1] The book is a Robinsonade that begins with the introduction of a self-sufficient but lonely hunter who misses his dead parents and longs for a companion. He gradually befriends a mermaid, and the story turns to consider her evolution as she comes to live with the hunter in his island cabin and learn the ways of the land. Despite his happiness, the hunter becomes troubled by dreams which the mermaid interprets as revealing his wish for a son, and his wish is soon answered: encountering a bear in the woods, the hunter is forced to defend himself and kills the bear and takes her cub home; seeing a lynx kitten that has strayed from its mother's cave, the hunter snatches it up and also brings it home; finally, a shipwrecked orphan is washed ashore in a boat along with the body of his dead mother and, in this way, the boy joins the other "sons" and the Animal Family is complete.

This was Jarrell's fourth children's book, written in 1963 directly after *Fly by Night* and composed, Mary Jarrell reports, in a fit of literary inspiration:

Something unexpected happened. After a false start or two, a book took hold of him and got written almost consecutively to its end. Daily, . . . it gathered up objects such as the deerskin rugs from Salzburg, the new window seat we had added to our house, the Gucci hunting horn over our brick hearth and our female satyr figurine from Amsterdam. Into this setting Randall put a bearded hunter and a mermaid, the lynx from the Washington Zoo, the seals from our Laguna [Beach, California] days, and finally gave these a boy who wanted to be adopted by *The Animal Family*.[2]

This, Jarrell's last book, also gathered up themes and characters from all his previous work. Indeed, *The Animal Family* is a triumphant culmination of Jarrell's poetry and novels. It could only have been written in a burst of sustained inspiration because, in all his work before it, Jarrell had already prepared himself for this.

Robinson Crusoe and mermaids had made their appearance in Jarrell's poems (e.g., "The Island" and "A Soul") collected in *The Seven League Crutches* (1951). These figures play an even more important part in Jarrell's later poetry—in poems like "The End of the Rainbow" (where mention is made of *Swiss Family Robinson* and mer-creatures) and more particularly in "Jamestown" (where "Nature is at last married to a man" when John Smith marries the female satyr Pocohantas). In fact, these later poems are collected in *The Woman at the Washington Zoo* (1962), a book whose central themes of loneliness and self-sufficiency seem to characterize the situation of the hunter at the opening of *The Animal Family.*

The figure of the animal-son had been anticipated even earlier. Jarrell had already compared bears and sons by 1945 in *Little Friend, Little Friend* in poems like "Second Air Force" and "Absent with Official Leave"; and the arrival of both the bear and the boy at the hunter's cabin after horrible storms had been presaged in "The Difficult Resolution" where Jarrell had spoken of emigrants coming, like implacable storms, to the log homes of America. Likewise, the lynx-son finds his predecessor in "Jerome" and the saint's friendship with his lion "son" and in the other animal friendships spoken of in *The Woman at the Washington Zoo*. In fact, *The Animal Family* can be said to answer a wish Mary Jarrell said her husband often expressed during the years they lived in Washington, D. C. (1956–1958): "A continual delight to us were the zoo stories and pictures from the *Washington Post*. We tore out and saved dozens of these. Randall particularly liked news about families who kept chimpanzees or ocelots or mountain lions. These often inspired him to say, 'Someday *we* ought to do that. Live somewhere where we could. . . .'"[3]

The boy of *The Animal Family* also recalls *The Woman at the Washington Zoo* and the intrepid boys pictured in its pages ("The Bronze David of Donatello" and "Nestus Gurley"). And he may simply be called the "boy" because, in writing his autobiographical poems for *The Lost World* (1965), Jarrell remembered that during his childhood year in Hollywood he used to play with Tawny, the lion featured in Tarzan movies. Like those Tarzan stories, *The Animal Family* is about a man in the wilderness who survives for a time on his own, happily encounters a female companion, lives with animals, and finally finds and adopts "Boy."

Besides his poetry, *The Animal Family* also gathered up Jarrell's children's books. The adoption of sons by the hunter and the mermaid echoes the adoption of the gingerbread son by the childless rabbit couple in *The Gingerbread Rabbit*. The mermaid's heroic venture from the sea to the *terra incognita* of the land recalls the bat-poet's daring as he leaves a nocturnal world behind and ventures into a sunlit world. But more than any other, *The Animal Family* most resembles the book that was written just before it, *Fly by Night.*

The central story-within-the-story of *Fly by Night,* "The Owl's Bedtime Story," tells of a lonely owlet who wishes for company, who hears in a dream the voice of a great owl promising him a companion, who leaves his nest and shyly meets another owlet, and who befriends this "sister" as they lurch back to his nest. *The Animal Family* begins with a lonely hunter who wishes for companions, who hears the voice of his dead mother in a dream, who leaves his cabin and shyly meets the mermaid, who befriends this "sister" who lurches onto the land and comes to live in his cabin. There is, however, a difference between the two books. "The Owl's Bedtime Story" is a really a dream that takes place inside the head of a lonely boy named David and it figures his wish for friends, but when he wakes there is no sister for him to find. But when the hunter wakes from his dream, the mermaid is really there and his wishes are fulfilled. As Jarrell says in the book's dedication, "Say what you like, but such things do happen—not often, but they do happen."

I

The Animal Family is a sequel to Kipling's *Jungle Books* and Burroughs's *Tarzan of the Apes.* The account of the boy Mowgli being raised by wolves—Jarrell observed in his essay "On Preparing to Read Kipling"—is essentially a story about parents and children: "To Kipling the world was a dark forest full of families; . . . [families] have so predominant a place in no other writer."[4] Influenced by Darwinian thought, Burroughs rewrote Kipling's story (in itself a revision of the myth of Romulus and Remus being raised by wolves) and had his hero raised by apes

and recorded Tarzan's ascent from the primeval jungle to western civilization; while the notion of the family remains the core
of the book, Burroughs yoked to it the idea of evolution.

Jarrell takes both these ideas to heart in *The Animal Family*
but enlarges the shared story in a mythic and archetypal fashion.

As the novel opens, we are introduced to "the hunter"; like
the other characters in the book (the mermaid, the bear, the
lynx, the boy) his name is emblematic, categorical, platonic. He
is a kind of Robinson Crusoe without a Friday, and Adam in
Eden with no Eve and all his ribs intact; he is all alone (his
parents are dead) and has no one to share his life with. One
night he dreams of his mother singing, and that voice melts into
another until he realizes he is hearing someone singing from off
the sea.

Enter the mermaid, an emigré from Hans Andersen's fairy
tale but without the bathetic wish for legs and for a soul that
mars Andersen's character. Over the course of many nights, in
a slow and patient way, the hunter befriends the shy mermaid.
They teach each other their languages, though the hunter is a
slower student of the watery, dolphin lingo. The mermaid is
fascinated by the "land that is so, so different" (20, 28), and the
hunter does his best to explain to her such perplexing things as
why someone might wish to come in out of the rain or the pur-
poses of a house, a bed, and a table. Despite the fact that the sea
people believe she is making a mistake, the mermaid finally
comes to the hunter's house and begins to live on the land.

Each of Jarrell's chapters advances with the introduction of
a new character and, having been presented with the hunter,
we turn now to consider the mermaid and her evolution. Like
some visitor from a foreign planet, the mermaid serves as a foil
and occasion for explaining the life of the land; and she tells him
of her own life under the sea. She is a kind of child who requires

explanations for the things adults take for granted: why we wear clothes, cook food, avoid getting too close to a fire. And, like a parent, the hunter patiently explains these things and teaches her nursery rhymes and tells her fairy tales.

But as she daily evolves, repeating the ontogeny of a child, it becomes clear that her role in this relationship changes into something different. They help each other "as a husband helps his wife" (37), even though the mermaid is a kind of spasmodic housekeeper and she sleeps in bed above the bearskin while he sleeps beneath it. As if to make clear their roles, the hunter carves for her a statue of his mother and a statue of his father; the mermaid observes: "She's like me!" and "There's no difference at all, [he's] just like you!" (50).

This idea is made clearer when the hunter has a troubling dream: he dreams of the old days when his parents were alive and sees himself in his father's shadow, the mermaid in his mother's shadow, but no one in his own childhood shadow. Playing the part of psychoanalyst, the mermaid interprets his dream and tells the hunter what he wishes for is a son so "it will all be the way it used to be" (61). But away out in the forest, there seems no way for them to "beg or borrow or steal a child" (61) to answer this dream.

Enter the bear. Hunting one night in the midst of a storm, the hunter comes between a bear and her cub and is forced to defend himself and kill the bear. He wraps the cub up and brings it home to present to the mermaid as their child. Like an infant, the bear is clumsy and awkward, eats everything, and sleeps a great deal. But he is good company even though, like a child, he must occasionally be disciplined: taught not to shake himself when he is wet, encouraged not to raid beehives if the bees follow him home. The family grows so content, it seems as if the bear had "lived with them always" (67). The bear, however, is only a partial answer to the hunter's dream-wish because he has to hibernate, and when he goes off to do just that the hunter once more feels the lack of a child.

Enter the lynx. The hunter finds a way to fill the void created by the hibernating bear when he spies a lynx cub that has strayed from its mother's cave and snatches it up. In a fashion, the lynx is an even better "child" than the bear; he is quick, lithe, skilled—"The bear's growing up had been one long accident; the lynx grew up as smoothly and designedly as he did everything else" (113). The difference between the two, in fact, mirrors the evolution of a child and presents a next step in child development: like a baby in its earliest years, the bear does little but eat and sleep; like a slightly older child, the lynx is playful and agile, and his table manners are far better than those of the bear. With the adoption of the lynx, the family unit comes closer to the hunter's wish that things "will be the way they used to be" when he was a boy. But not close enough.

Enter the boy. Exploring one day near the shore, the lynx comes across a shipwrecked child who has been washed ashore in a boat with the body of his dead mother. Following the animal home, the boy comes to the cabin and falls asleep. The hunter and mermaid are surprised to discover him. His mother's corpse is buried, and the boy is adopted.

The boy represents another stage in childhood development reached in steps by the mermaid, the bear and then the lynx; and he importantly reminds the hunter of the way he was when he was a child. In a fatherly way, the hunter teaches his new son the way he was taught, about hunting and bows and arrows. The mermaid teaches him to swim and speak the dolphins' language. Though they tell the boy that the lynx (not the stork) brought him, it seems to all of them that he has been with them "always" (180). In this repetition of the generations, the hunter's wish is answered—the Animal Family is complete; things

102

have evolved to the way they used to be, the way families have always been.

II

"I didn't want to illustrate *The Animal Family* at all," Sendak told me. "In fact, that was the only time I got close to an argument with Jarrell because he was hurt; he thought I didn't like the book. I loved the book. I just felt he didn't need me. If you had drawn the mermaid dragging herself . . . it would have been so vulgar. Whereas, just the image of her, his image of her, is poetic. But you can't draw her. You couldn't draw the child. You couldn't draw the hunter."

Informed of Sendak's decision and saddened, Jarrell decided to "illustrate" the books with nature photography—with pictures of the Oregon and California coastal landscape that had inspired the book—and Jarrell and his wife pored over collections of photographs by Ansel Adams and Edward Weston. Still not satisfied, Jarrell appealed to his editor, Michael di Capua, who took the appeal to Sendak and proposed that Sendak "decorate" the book. That was a solution that pleased the artist; and when the book appeared, its title page would read: "The Animal Family / by Randall Jarrell / Decorations by / Maurice Sendak."

Sendak's task, as he saw it, was "to illustrate the book without illustrating it." If he couldn't draw the mermaid and the hunter and the child, he could at least "draw the place where they lived." And so, Sendak fashioned a picture to precede each of the book's chapters: "little stage settings, like overtures for each chapter." To do so, Sendak drew upon the powers he was later to employ in his career as a set designer for such celebrated performances as the Houston Opera Company's *The Magic Flute* (1980) and the Pacific Northwest Ballet's *The*

Nutcracker Suite (1983). He would provide the environment, the ambience for Jarrell's story.

Sendak's coastal landscapes do recall Ansel Adams's and Edward Weston's photographs of the Pacific Northwest "from Coos Bay, Oregon, to Big Sur, California."[5] And like Whitman's "Out of the Cradle Endlessly Rocking," this seashore is extravagant in its haunting loneliness. The picture for the opening of the first chapter introduces this land "where the forest runs down to the ocean" (5). Since the view is from off the water, it implies the approach of the mermaid to the shore. And in the lower left corner can be seen the hunter's solitary cabin, what will be her resting place after the mermaid courageously makes her slow and hesitant way onto the land (Figure 20).

The point of view changes in Sendak's picture for the beginning of the second chapter; instead of the land viewed from the sea, the sea is now viewed from the land. The mermaid has now come ashore and lives with the hunter, and they can look out and observe a tranquil sea under moonlit skies (Figure 21).

The picture for the third chapter is somewhere farther up in the land than the shoreline in the picture before. The hunter has been troubled by the dreams which reveal his wish for a son, but there is no way for the mermaid and him to make one. In the third chapter, the hunter finds and adopts the bear cub—grafts a son on to this otherwise barren relationship. And Sendak pictures this, marvelously, as an old tree stump on which new growth appears and blossoms (Figure 22).

The fourth chapter begins with a picture of the cave where the bear has retreated for his winter's hibernation. The mermaid fears the bear has gone into the cave and died, and the monumental granite has a funereal tone; but the hunter reassures her that the bear is only sleeping, and the blooming verdure upon the rocks seems to offer Sendak's same assurance (Figure 23). About this picture Sendak has said, "Some readers

·I·
THE   HUNTER

Figure 20

·II·
THE MERMAID

Figure 21

· III ·

THE HUNTER BRINGS HOME A BABY

Figure 22

·IV·
THE BEAR

Figure 23

claim to see animals and other creatures, even people, but nothing of the kind is there."[6] Despite his conviction, the outline on the right does resemble a bear's profile and in the entrance to the cave lies what might be taken as the form of a human child.

Sendak did not choose to picture any living things in the illustrations he created for the book; instead, he observed, "These were my personal landscapes of what Jarrell was talking about."[7] In a deep, unconscious fashion the landscapes are full of archetypal images. The picture that opens chapter 5 is an example of this. There, Sendak presents a vision of a mountainous, seaside cliff with trees growing on it (Figure 24).

Anticipating Jungian typology, the ancient Chinese—in their lexicon of archetypal images, *The I-Ching*—believed that something quite distinct and universal was represented by the image of the tree-on-the-mountain: "Gradual Development. . . . The tree on the mountain . . . does not shoot up like a swamp plant; its growth proceeds gradually [as a courtship that eventually leads to marriage or a pregnancy which comes to full term]."[8] What better image is there than Sendak's, then, for this story of a hunter who slowly courts a mermaid, of a family which gradually develops around them?

Archetypal imagery appears in other pictures. In countless mythologies, the cave and the sea serve as symbols for the Other World where we go when we die, where we come from when we are born. It seems no coincidence, then, that Sendak's picture of the cave for chapter 4 is balanced by another which opens chapter 6, where what is seen is the boat that has washed ashore with the shipwrecked boy (Figure 25). Just as the mermaid fears the bear has "died" when he goes into the cave, the boy is "born" into the Animal Family when he is washed ashore from the amniotic sea—or, as Lucretius says, "Behold the infant: Like a shipwrecked sailor, cast ashore by the fury of the

·V·
THE LYNX

Figure 24

·VI·
THE LYNX
&
THE BEAR
BRING HOME
A BOY

Figure 25

billows, the poor child lies naked on the ground, after Nature has dragged him in pain from the mother's womb."⁹

With the boy's arrival the Animal Family is complete. In the time before that, the lonely hunter's life had been barren and sterile. The mermaid's companionship is satisfying for a time, but without children something was missing. The bear and the lynx carry things further but only partially fill this void. When the boy comes to them, however, what has been sought is finally achieved: another family has arisen to carry on; a line of continuity is established from the time when the hunter was a son and his parents alive, to the time now when the hunter has himself become a parent and the boy his son. Sendak pictures this new generation arising out of the old in his picture that opens chapter 7: again an old tree blooming with new life, and at its base are the bow and arrows the hunter has fashioned for the boy, like those the hunter had played with when he was young (Figure 26).

In this subtle way, then, by implication and suggestion, Sendak "decorated" *The Animal Family*. But he did not stop there. The very book itself, he explained, was a part of his encompassing decoration of the story:

> The shape and the design of the book is very square. I know how desperately Randall needed a family. That's the whole message of everything he wrote—this incredible *need* for a family—and so, I wanted to give him a fat, square, little book. And if you'll notice, the type is in the middle of the page with a great "island" of white space around it [Figure 27]. That's for coziness and hugging. So, you have these little pieces of type, big margins, and thick boards—we got triple thick boards for the binding—so it's almost like a house, like opening a door instead of a book [Figure 28]. You see, I wanted to illustrate it not just with these opening pictures, but with the whole shape, smell, and design of the

112

·VII·
THE
BOY

Figure 26

of her own words, and then asked im-
patiently: "You have legs, I have not
legs. The moon is white, the sky is black.
What is that?"

"Different?"

"Different! Different! The land is
different."

Sometimes the land was so different
that the mermaid would learn a word in
a few seconds and after a half-hour's
explanation still not know what it
meant. One day—the mermaid came to
the beach in the daytime, now—the
hunter pointed up over the meadow and
said, in the clear divided tones of a
teacher making something plain: "That
is my *house.*"

20

Figure 27

"House," hissed the mermaid.
"House."

"I sleep in the *house,* on a *bed.* I eat
in the *house,* on a *table.*"

"Bed," said the mermaid. "Table."
But her quick eyes looked strained and
hesitant; it was plain that she had no
idea what the hunter was talking about.

The hunter started cheerfully, "A
table's a big flat thing with legs"—the
mermaid's eyes brightened: she knew
what legs meant, and felt very landish
for knowing—"that you eat on."

"Why do you get on it to eat?"

"Oh no, *you* don't get on it, you put
what you're going to eat on it."

"Why?"

21

Figure 28

book. It would look like his little family. It would be a gift
for Randall—his home, finally, inside that book. I love that
book. In terms of illustrating a book without illustrating it,
that's a very good example.

Sendak worked with his favorite book designer, Atha
Tehon, to create this special volume for his friend. He did so
because of his fond feelings for and admiration of Jarrell: "I've
worked with many writers, but he was probably the most extraordinary of them all, because he was a poet and had a vision-
ary sense. But, oddly for a writer, he also had a graphic sense, so
that he knew what a book could look like. Yet he never dictated
to me what it should look like. Randall conceived of the book
whole, from its binding to the quality of the paper, so working
with him was an amazing experience."[10]

III

On October 14, 1965, while walking along a road in Chapel
Hill, North Carolina, Randall Jarrell was struck and killed by a
car. Members of the family and others have strenuously argued
that the event was an accident and that the facts clearly indicate
this. Others, aware that Jarrell had been despondent and under
treatment for emotional problems, have concluded that it was a
suicide. As Suzanne Ferguson suggests, this is now the more
commonly held belief because (in a process akin to legend formation) biography has been subsumed by mythology and Jarrell
has been dragooned to serve as one more example of the romantic "doomed poet" of a "doomed generation."[11]
    In light of these circumstances, some critics have tended to
approach Jarrell's later work in a tragic fashion and to hunt for
clues of a "turning down toward finality" which would permit
an easy grouping of Jarrell with such poet-suicides as John Ber-

ryman and Sylvia Plath. *The Animal Family,* Jarrell's last children's book, does not lend itself to this kind of *ad hominem* distortion. Instead, it is a happy book; despite the struggles beneath its surface, it ends with unqualified success.

More than any of Jarrell's other books for children, *The Animal Family* triumphs. It remedies the shortcomings of the previous books—their unresolved conclusions and ambivalent portraits of mothers. What lies behind these is suggested in Jarrell's comments on Kipling's stories. After noting that Kipling spent six traumatic years when he was separated from his parents at their insistence, Jarrell turns to consider the author's fiction:

> To Kipling the world was a dark forest full of families; so that when your father and mother leave you in the forest to die, the wolves that come . . . are always Father Wolf and Mother Wolf, your real father and your real mother, and you are—as not even the little wolves ever quite are—their real son. The family romance, the two families of the Hero, have so predominant a place in no other writer. . . . Kipling's Daemon kept bringing Kipling stories in which the wild animals turn out to be Mowgli's real father and mother, a heathen Lama turns out to be the orphaned Kim's real father. . . . This is all very absurd, all very pathetic? Oh yes, that's very likely; but, reader, down in the darkness, where the wishes sleep, snuggled together like bats, you and I are [Baby Wolf, Mowgli, and Kim, too].[12]

Jarrell goes on to argue that Kipling's second families were an answer to his pain and that it was a pain Kipling never acknowledged; he "never said a word or thought a thought against his parents." This avoidance, Jarrell believes, is behind the dissatisfaction readers sometimes feel with Kipling's sunny worlds: "As it was, his world had been torn in two and he himself torn in two; for under the part of him that extenuated everything, blamed for nothing, there was certainly a part that extenuated nothing, blamed for everything—a part whose existence he never admitted, most especially to himself." There are only a few Kipling stories, Jarrell pointedly notes, that "have a witch for Hansel to push in the oven."[13]

These remarks are not only a keen explanation of the short-comings of Kipling's stories, but of Jarrell's children's books as well. Like Kipling's, Jarrell's stories feature the second family: this is clear in the gingerbread rabbit's adoption by the real rabbits and in David's adoption by the owl; though it is less obvious in *The Bat-Poet*, one phrase in Jarrell's remarks on Kipling (". . . where the wishes sleep, snuggled together like bats") suggests a resemblance between the desire for reunion with parents in Kipling's stories and the young bat's return to the snuggling companionship of the other bats. But more important is Jarrell's identification of the source of reader dissatisfaction with Kipling's stories: a determined avoidance of unflattering portraits of parents and a constant denial of hostile feelings toward them. This also explains something about Jarrell's stories.

Fathers, notably, have a small role in the children's books, which primarily focus on the mother-son nexus. The rabbit-father has a small part in *The Gingerbread Rabbit* and, as a rescuer, is clearly the opposite of the threatening, male fox; extensive textual similarities, however, suggest the fox is a double for Mary's mother. Mary's father is not mentioned at all. In *Fly by Night*, David does see an oedipal dream over his father's head and the owlet in "The Owl's Bedtime Story" is given advice by a paternal "great owl," but on the whole fathers are given short shrift and the emphasis and basis of this nocturnal fantasy is David's relationship with his mother.

The general insignificance of fathers might be explained thematically (oedipal rivalry does not interest Jarrell as much as separation anxiety, where maternal relations are conspicuous)

119

or biographically (after his parents separated when he was eleven, Jarrell was raised by his mother). Whatever the case, the avoidance of this topic is evident in Jarrell's inability to speak about fathers—most revealing, perhaps, in a small scene in *The Bat-Poet*. The only time the bat-poet is unable to compose a poem is when he tries to create a verse portrait of the markedly paternal cardinal:

> All the next day he watched the cardinal. . . . While the cardinal was cracking the seed his two babies stood underneath him on tiptoe, fluttering their wings and quivering all over, their mouths wide open. . . . The father was such a beautiful clear bright red, with his tall crest the wind rippled like fur, that it didn't seem right for him to be so harried and useful and hard-working: it was like seeing a general in a red uniform washing hundreds and hundreds of dishes. . . . But it was no use: no matter how much the bat watched, he never got an idea. Finally he went to the chipmunk and said in a perplexed voice: "I can't make up a poem about the cardinal. . . . I would if I could," the bat said, "but I can't. I don't know why I can't, but I can't." (24–25)

Mothers play far more conspicuous roles in the children's books, but in them Jarrell practices avoidance in another fashion: he always paints mothers in a flattering light and often assigns everything that is unflattering to some other character. Like Kipling, he extenuates; or, to say it differently, he engages in "loving hypocrisy"—what Jarrell confesses to doing in his poem "The Lost World" when he wishes to "explain away" what he found disturbing when Mama wrung the chicken's neck. The mothers in *The Gingerbread Rabbit* (the mother who bakes him, the rabbit-mother who adopts him) may be misunderstood but they are loving; it is their obvious counterpart, the fox, that is malevolent. The bat-mother in *The Bat-Poet* is loving; it is her double, the other explorer of the night, the owl, who is threatening. So, too, the mothers in *Fly by Night* (David's mother, the owl) are loving; it is the dog and the cat who feature the other side of the mother, who cause those feelings of uneasiness that are denied. Until *The Animal Family*, then, Jarrell can be said to excuse and avoid those issues he believed Kipling excused and avoided. And like Kipling's, Jarrell's stories notably lack "a witch for Hansel to push in the oven."

In this regard, there is something strikingly different about *The Animal Family*: it is a predominately male story (there is only one female and she is an asexual mermaid) and a tale littered with dead or absent mothers (the hunter's mother is dead when the story opens, the bear's mother is killed, the lynx is stolen from his mother, and when the boy is washed ashore in the lifeboat he is accompanied by the corpse of his mother). In a way yet to be explained and only suggested by these circumstances, a break with the biological mother seems to be a necessary prerequisite to membership in the Animal Family.

To begin to understand this, it is worth recalling one of Jarrell's observations about Kipling: "The family romance, the two families of the Hero, have so predominant a place in no other writer." By this comment, Jarrell draws on his psychoanalytic expertise to suggest that Kipling's stories may be understood in terms of Freud's concept of the "family romance," a concept most clearly articulated in Otto Rank's famous essay "The Myth of the Birth of the Hero."

In that essay, Rank observes:

> The detachment of the growing individual from the authority of the parents is one of the most necessary, but also one of the most painful achievements of evolution. It is absolutely essential for this detachment to take place, and it may be assumed that all normal grown individuals have accom-

121

> plished it to a certain extent. . . . On the other hand, there
> exists a class of neurotics whose conditions indicate that
> they have failed to solve this problem.[14]

This central passage in Rank's essay is, in a fashion, a summary of the issues of *The Animal Family*. This can be clearly seen in three characters in Jarrell's book—the mermaid, the hunter, and the boy—and in the way they face the sometimes painful detachment from their biological parents, the detachment Rank finds necessary for "evolution."

The mermaid's new allegiance to the Animal Family involves a painful and heroic decision to leave the sea behind and live on the land. In making this choice to push on to the new, she willingly accepts tension and trauma. She must leave the sea and, like a child, evolve—learn a language, what a house and bed are for, what a nursery rhyme is about. She must, in other words, become civilized.

Civilization, Freud has observed, brings its discontents, and the mermaid's decision to live on the land brings her a full measure of these. One example of this can be found early in the book when the hunter wonders, "Do mermaids cry?" (52). The question arises because, in the beginning of their friendship, the mermaid shares the indifference of the sea people to all events; the hunter is surprised, for example, by the mermaid's nonchalant attitude towards her sister's death. But as she comes to live on the land, she becomes civilized; she develops an emotional or psychic life, becomes attached to others, learns what boredom is, and experiences discontents. At the end of the book the hunter witnesses the answer to his question: "The mermaid could cry" (171).

The mermaid's decision to push on to the new is not only painful, it is also heroic. The sea is attractive to her because under the waves she can retreat from the troubles of the land to the placid indifference she says can be found there: "When it storms for the people, no matter how terribly it storms, the storm isn't real—swim down a few strokes and it's calm there, down there it's always calm. And death is no different, if it's someone else who dies. We say, 'Swim away from it'; we swim away from everything" (170). But the mermaid forgoes the sea and pushes on to live on the land. She does not regress to the sea but evolves from it.

In various mythologies the sea is thought of as the matrix, the womb; it is the origin (the sea people say, "everything good comes from the sea"), and it is the end of things (the mermaid remarks, "in the end everything comes to us [in the sea]"). In Jarrell's poetry the sea also represents the matriarchal realm from which beings come and to which they return: it is the "amniotic sea," the "womb—the waves of constriction, the rejecting lips / Wet still with the tides that formed us, . . . that blind mother . . . that gives and takes away."[15]

To come from the sea is to embark on a new life. To return to the sea is to die or regress. In making her new allegiance to the Animal Family, the mermaid has not only decided for the land, but also broken with her biological past; she forswears any regressive desire to return to the amniotic security of the sea and passionately declares her preference for the land.

It is hard to underestimate the importance of this new heroic portrait in Jarrell's work. It is a genuine accomplishment in light of Jarrell's previous children's books. While the gingerbread rabbit and the bat-poet and the owlet in *Fly by Night* make heroic decisions to go out into the new world and suffer many pains doing so, in the end they are all overcome by regressive desires and return to the warm and hibernating and maternal worlds they have left. The mermaid, on the other hand, except for some initial homesickness, breaks with her biological past; and her new life is not terminated by some final regressive return to that salty world from which she has come.

While the mermaid is able to break with her biological past, the case of the hunter is more complicated. This is revealed when, as the Animal Family forms around him, the hunter is troubled by dreams and thoughts about his dead parents.

The injunction of *Genesis*—"A man shall leave his parents and cleave unto his wife"—speaks of the formation of one kind of allegiance in terms of a break with the biological past. A satisfactory break with the parents, Rank suggests, opens up the possibility of evolution. This may explain why so many mothers are "cashiered" in *The Animal Family* and why the hunter seems to have a role in all these events: the hunter steals the lynx from his mother, the bear's mother is killed by the hunter, and the boy is washed ashore with the corpse of his mother which the hunter buries.

Read in a psychological fashion, the hunter's disposing of so many mothers symbolizes something quite healthy—the dissolution of the parental bond necessary for evolution. On the other hand, psychologists would observe, the hunter's break with his parents is only a partial one since it is symbolically mitigated: his own mother is already dead and, if he dissolves the parental bond, he does so only by disposing of others' mothers. The question remains, in other words, whether the hunter, in forming *his own* allegiance to the Animal Family, makes a satisfactory break with his parents or joins instead that group described by Rank—"a class of neurotics whose conditions indicate that they have failed to solve this problem."

In fact, the hunter seems to go through a three-step process, most evident in his reactions to memories of his parents. Each of these steps recalls the different ways memories are employed in *The Lost World:* 1) in some poems (e.g., "The Lost World") Jarrell thinks of his childhood with nostalgia and acknowledges how much he misses the past; 2) in others, however, memory is something that infects the present (the narrator of "Hope," for example, confesses he has an oedipal obsession that prevents him from regarding his wife in some other way than as his mother); and 3) in still other poems (e.g., "Thinking of the Lost World") Jarrell seems to move to the happier conclusion that the past is never lost but provides the originals or archetypes upon which later events improvise variations.

Early in *The Animal Family* it seems that the hunter has never fully broken the bond with his dead parents. He is constantly troubled by dreams about them, carves statues of them. Even when he teaches the mermaid a nursery rhyme he learned in his childhood, she can see something come over him: "Whenever anything reminded the hunter of his father and mother, you could see that he missed them and longed to have them alive again" (51).

Near the middle of the book, something else can be noticed. As his friendship with the mermaid grows, he begins to see her as a replication of his dead mother. When the narrator says she helps him like a "wife," the hunter says: "You're as good a cook as my mother" (37). When he carves a statue of his mother the mermaid observes, "Why, she's like me"; and when he carves a statue of his father she notes, "It's just like you!" (50). And later when he dreams of his dead parents, he sees himself in his father's shadow and the mermaid in his mother's (59–60).

Like the poem "Hope" (with its confessions of oedipal fixations by a narrator who wishes he could see his wife as someone other than his mother), these resemblances and replications may suggest that the hunter has not outgrown the Oedipus Complex but only re-envisioned it; with the statues and the dreams the oedipal wish is, in a sense, fulfilled: the hunter takes his father's place. This leaves the mermaid, of course, in the anomalous position she has in this tale as both the hunter's symbolic "wife" and symbolic "mother"; and this symbology must be maintained because of the sexual taboos implied in the Oedipus Complex: the relationship with the wife-mother must be chaste and the symbology preserves this. It is worth noting, in this regard, that what the hunter considers the best gift the mermaid has brought him from the sea is a ship's figurehead of a beautiful woman with hooved legs like that of a goat or deer and whose "blue eyes stared out past you at something far away" (40). The anatomical description fits the mythical personage known in classical times as *Fauna,* sometimes called *Bona Mater,* who was noted for her uncompromising chastity since her eyes never fell on another man after her marriage. But it is, perhaps, more important to note that, among all the characters of the book (the hunter, the bear, the lynx, the boy), the mermaid is the *only* fantastical creature; the genital-less anatomy of this wife-mother defuses any note of sexuality in the hunter's oedipal relationship with the mermaid.

In this way, *The Animal Family* is a tremendously complicated *male* fantasy. While explanations can be offered for the symbolic matricides in terms of the resolution of separation anxiety, these multiple events in the early portions of the book might also be seen to reveal a pronounced anti-feminine attitude. At the same time and in counterpoint, the very same pages are full of a loving portrait of the mermaid, the hunter's frequent estimations that her skills far exceed his own, and the consistent use of feminine or matriarchal symbology by a poet whose frequent and sympathetic portraits of women has often been noted. In this regard, the mermaid seems the only genuine hero of the tale as she goes through her painful and dramatic evolution. Still, that progress is, to some extent, "arrested"; unlike Andersen's mermaid, she never acquires legs and seems a "crippled" figure on the land. She is "arrested" in another way by her lack of sexuality. Jarrell may have felt the need to desexualize her because this was a children's book, but the hunter is not the same age as the owlet in *Fly by Night* whose years explain why he sees the companion he acquires as a "sister" and a "friend." Instead, the lack of a grown-up relationship with the mermaid suggests how the hunter's difficulties with his parental bond have resulted in an immature vision of women: they may be a "sister" or "friend" or even a "daughter," but to serve a male's psychological needs they must never grow—as Mary Jarrell puts it—"into a Wife or Mother."

It is only near the end of the book, with the introduction of the boy, that the hunter finally makes a satisfactory break with his parents. When the hunter has his last troubling dream, the mermaid once again interprets it: "I know what your dream means. It means you want a boy to live with us. Then you'll be your father's shadow, and I'll be your mother's, and the boy will be yourself the way you used to be" (60–61). The clumsy bear cub is a partial answer to this wish, the lithe lynx kitten even better, but with the addition of the shipwrecked boy the wish is finally fulfilled. The present becomes a variation upon past archetypes, so that the hunter and the mermaid can honestly and platonically say that it seems as if the boy has been with them "always" (180). From the moment the boy enters the story, the hunter has no more troubling dreams about his parents, nor does he view the mermaid as his mother incarnate. Simply put, his break with his parents is complete once he becomes a parent himself.

In his portrait of the mermaid Jarrell shows how she heroically breaks with her biological past and evolves. The hunter's relationship with his past is more complex and has to be painfully worked through to its resolution. There is, however, one character in the book who has an unproblematic relationship to these issues that concern the mermaid and the hunter.

Only the boy escapes pain, unlike the mermaid whose pain comes from her decision to push on to the new or the hunter whose pain comes from his troubled thoughts about the past. While the mermaid passionately argues as the book concludes that the sea is "not for me! . . . No, the land's better! The land's better!" (169–71)—the boy accepts his new life without declarative fervor: "If one day as he played at the edge of the forest some talking bird had flown down and asked him: 'Do you like your life?' he would not have known what to say, but would have asked the bird: 'Can you not like it?'" (162). While the hunter is troubled by dreams and thoughts about his dead parents, "except for one or two confused, uneasy dreams" (156), the boy is not troubled by the loss of his own mother and has no problem accepting his allegiance to the Animal Family.

The boy comes mysteriously over the sea and to the land as an answer to the prayers of the Animal Family. He is, in the words of the mermaid, "so new" yet he seems to have lived with them "always." He is both the New Child and the *Puer Aeternus* who has risen above painful choosings and transcended a biological past. He takes the virgin mermaid as his "mother," the terrestial hunter as his "father," and the Animal Family as his "family" with the same sublimity of Christ when he said: "'Who is my mother? Who are my brothers?' and stretching out his hands to his disciples said, 'Behold my mother and my brothers.'"[16]

IV

The Animal Family presents the fruition of Jarrell's thoughts upon a central theme of his prose and poetry—separation anxiety and its resolution. This becomes even clearer with hindsight.

Jarrell's earliest book of poetry, *Blood for a Stranger* (1942), is full of haunting portraits of childhood loneliness and of a child missing its mother; while there are poems that speak of the opposite emotion, the desire to escape a parent, in those willful separation is shown to bring even more pain. The war poetry of *Little Friend, Little Friend* (1945) is strikingly different: it stresses that separation is a natural and existential condition (since all have been rejected by the indifferent matriarchy of the universe); and the poems condemn those who evade (as the title of one poem puts it) "The Difficult Resolution," those who refuse to accept their existential separateness and wish instead to regress to "amniotic" security. *Losses* (1948) shows individuals who have made this "difficult resolution" but also acknowledges that even when the separateness of child from mother is accepted, issues can still remain unresolved; even after the death of the mother, Jarrell suggests in "Orestes at Tauris," separation anxiety may grow more aggravated and bring with it pain and reprisals from maternal forces beyond the grave. In *The Seven-League Crutches* (1958) Jarrell's characters wrestle with this Other from beyond the grave, but in "A Quilt Pattern" the Other-mother is finally disposed of: separation anxiety is finally resolved in this poem's dream re-enactment of the symbolic matricide of "Hansel and Gretel."

"A Quilt Pattern" can be viewed as a milestone in Jarrell's wrestling with the theme of separation anxiety. This may, in fact, be why Jarrell himself considered it the best of his dream poems and credited it with a "happy ending."[17] Its happy ending is notable because such a resolution is rare in Jarrell's previous work. But while Jarrell did turn a corner with "A Quilt Pattern," it was not his last word upon the subject.

Karl Shapiro once suggested that if Jarrell's corpus ever required a subtitle, a most suitable one would be "Hansel and Gretel in America."[18] In fact, the poems of *The Woman at the Washington Zoo* (1960) can be said to concern themselves with what Hansel and Gretel might have felt after they disposed of mother in "A Quilt Pattern"—with self-sufficiency and lone-liness, with making a family of their own. The thought of fami-lies seems to have sent Jarrell back to memories of his own childhood in *The Lost World* (1965), but in a poem like "Hope" the narrator confesses that, despite his family life, he has not been able to rid himself of obsessive thoughts about mothers. Another poem in the book hints at the same kind of backsliding: "The House in the Woods" can be viewed as a retreat from the position of "A Quilt Pattern" because, while it also makes use of the story of "Hansel and Gretel," it does not present a salutary matricide but a desire to be cradled in the witch's arms.

This last poem suggests a good deal about Jarrell's first three children's books. None ends in a salutary matricide. They often conclude, instead, with the fulfillment of the wish to be cradled in the witch's arms: having escaped various mother-fig-ures in the woods, the gingerbread rabbit finds a home with another when he is adopted by the real rabbits; after heroically putting some distance between himself and the other less daring bats, the bat-poet balks and returns to warm, maternal security; seeing the necessity to "leave the nest," the owlet in *Fly by Night* does so but returns to his mother and she folds her wings around him.

In light of all this, *The Animal Family* is a tale that speaks of the resolution of separation anxiety and a success that rivals "A Quilt Pattern," and it presents a triumph that will make the book a classic in the canon of children's literature. Unlike the characters in the previous children's books, the mermaid does not enjoy just a brief interlude of independence that terminates in a regressive return to the womb; she breaks with the original, salty, amniotic world and evolves. The hunter, too, though he is initially troubled by memories of the past, finally exchanges the worries of a child for those of a parent. But it is in the boy of *The Animal Family* that Jarrell finds a complete answer—a contented heart that cannot imagine how it might be otherwise.

Notes

Preface

1. Fiedler, "Jarrell's Criticism: A Footnote," 66–69.

2. "An Unread Book" prefaced the 1965 reissue of Christina Stead's *The Man Who Loved Children* (New York: Holt, Rinehart and Winston); the essay was reprinted in Jarrell's *The Third Book of Criticism*, 3–54.

3. See, for example, "On Preparing to Read Rudyard Kipling," the introduction to *The Best Stories of Rudyard Kipling*, ed. Randall Jarrell (Garden City, N.Y.: Hanover House, 1961); reprinted in Jarrell's *Kipling, Auden and Co.*, 332–45.

4. M. L. Rosenthal, "Randall Jarrell" in *American Writers: A Collection of Literary Biographies*, ed. Leonard Uber (New York: Charles Scribner's Sons, 1974), 2:367.

5. Watson, "Randall Jarrell: The Last Years," 264.

6. Shapiro, "The Death of Randall Jarrell," 223.

7. Dickey, "Randall Jarrell," 48.

8. Lowell, "Randall Jarrell," 109.

9. Ransom, "The Rugged Way of Genius," 176.

10. Mary Jarrell, "The Group of Two," 295.

11. Cott, *Pipers at the Gates of Dawn*, xiv–xvi.

Chapter One

1. *Randall Jarrell's Letters,* 460.
2. Cf. Bettelheim, *The Uses of Enchantment,* 159–66.
3. *The Complete Poems,* 292.
4. Blount, *Animal Land;* Chesterton, "The Ethics of Elfland."

Chapter Two

1. The Swiss scholar Helen Hagenbüchle (author of *The Black Goddess: A Study of the Archetypal Feminine in the Poetry of Randall Jarrell*) made this observation in a letter to me.
2. Mary Jarrell, "Note" to Caedmon recording of Jarrell reading *The Bat-Poet.*
3. Mary Jarrell, "Ideas and Poems," 218.
4. Mary Jarrell, "The Group of Two," 290.
5. Hawthorne's Owen Warland is not a bat and a poet, but a watchmaker and an artist. He gives up repairing watches and the company of others to stay up all night to work on his art—not poems, but a device that will embody the beautiful. Two males in Hawthorne's story (another watchmaker and a blacksmith) are as uncomprehending as bats and as critical as mockingbirds—they deride Owen's artistic endeavors. But Owen believes there is one person who sympathetically understands his art—his chipmunk, Annie Hovenden. He realizes he is mistaken, however, when Annie finally gives her hand not to the "queer" Owen, but to the burly blacksmith. This event throws Owen back on himself, but he finally recovers enough to complete his device of beauty and then returns to present it to others. They are not asleep, hanging upside down on a rafter, but they are uncomprehending and the device is accidentally destroyed. Owen's sole satisfaction, at the end of the tale, is having accomplished something for himself.
6. *Randall Jarrell's Letters,* 482–83.
7. Mary Jarrell, "Note" to Caedmon recording of *The Bat-Poet.*
8. Shapiro, "The Death of Randall Jarrell," 206–7, 213.

9. Mary Jarrell, "Note" to Caedmon recording of *The Bat-Poet*.

10. Neumeyer, "Randall Jarrell's *The Bat-Poet*"; Nodelman, "The Craft or Sullen Art of a Mouse and a Bat."

11. Griswold and Burness, "The Art of Fiction," 221.

12. Shapiro, "The Death of Randall Jarrell," 223.

13. *The Complete Poems*, 309.

14. Cited in Wright, *Randall Jarrell: A Descriptive Bibliography*, 92.

15. Ibid.

16. Several years later, John Schoenherr illustrated one of the poems of *The Bat-Poet* (titled "Bats" when it appeared in Jarrell's *The Lost World*) in a series of pictures that appeared as a children's book titled *A Bat is Born* (New York: Macmillan, 1978).

17. Lanes, *The Art of Maurice Sendak*, 135.

Chapter Three

1. *Randall Jarrell's Letters*, 463.

2. Updike, "Randall Jarrell Writing Stories for Children," 57–60.

3. Lanes, *The Art of Maurice Sendak*, 201.

4. Cited in Hagenbüchle, *The Black Goddess*, 20–21.

5. Updike, "Randall Jarrell Writing Stories for Children," 57–58.

6. *Kipling, Auden, and Co.*, 334.

7. Mary Jarrell, "Introduction" to *Jerome: The Biography of a Poem*, 13.

Chapter Four

1. Travers, "A Kind of Visitation," 55–57.

2. Mary Jarrell, "The Group of Two," 296–97.

3. Mary Jarrell, "Introduction" to *Jerome*, 12.

4. *Kipling, Auden, and Co.*, 344.

5. Mary Jarrell, "The Animal Family," 24.

6. Lanes, *The Art of Maurice Sendak*, 138.

7. Ibid.

8. *The I Ching or Chinese Book of Changes*, trans. Richard Wilhelm and Cary F. Banes (Princeton: Princeton University Press, 1967), 204–8.

9. Cited in Rank, "*The Myth of the Birth of the Hero*," 73 (n. 8).

10. Lanes, *The Art of Maurice Sendak*, 128.

11. Ferguson, "The Death of Randall Jarrell: A Problem in Legendary Biography." Cf. Meyers, "The Death of Randall Jarrell."

12. *Kipling, Auden, and Co.*, 344–45.

13. Ibid., 341, 344.

14. Rank, *The Myth of the Birth of the Hero*, 67–68.

15. *Collected Poems*, 398–400.

16. Matthew 12:47–50.

17. *Letters*, 302–4.

18. Stanley Kunitz repeats this remark in "Out of the Cage," 100.

Selected Bibliography

The most comprehensive bibliography of works by Randall Jarrell is Stuart Wright's *Randall Jarrell: A Descriptive Bibliography, 1929–1983* (Charlottesville: University Press of Virginia, 1986). The most recent bibliography of works about Randall Jarrell is Jeffrey Meyers' "Randall Jarrell: A Bibliography of Criticism, 1941–1981," *Bulletin of Bibliography* 39 (Summer 1982):227–34. The bibliography which follows is by no means a complete record of all the works and sources I have consulted. Instead, it is intended to serve as a convenience for those who wish to pursue the study of Jarrell's children's books; other relevant works mentioned in this study are also listed here. Two collections of essays are referred to in this bibliography by short title. *RJ, 1914–1965* indicates essays appearing in Robert Lowell, Peter Taylor, and Robert Penn Warren, eds., *Randall Jarrell: 1914–1965* (New York: Farrar, Straus and Giroux, 1967). Similarly, *"Critical Essays"* indicates essays in Suzanne Ferguson, ed., *Critical Essays on Randall Jarrell* (Boston: Hall, 1983).

Selected Bibliography

Original Works by Randall Jarrell

The Animal Family. Decorations by Maurice Sendak. New York: Pantheon Books, 1965.

The Bat-Poet. Pictures by Maurice Sendak. New York: Macmillan, 1964.

The Complete Poems of Randall Jarrell. New York: Farrar, Straus, and Giroux, 1969.

Fly by Night. Pictures by Maurice Sendak. New York: Farrar, Straus and Giroux, 1976.

The Gingerbread Rabbit. Pictures by Garth Williams. New York: Macmillan, 1964.

Jerome: The Biography of a Poem. Edited by Mary Jarrell. New York: Grossman, 1971.

Kipling, Auden and Co.: Essays and Reviews 1935–1964. New York: Farrar, Straus and Giroux, 1980.

The Lost World: Last Poems. Foreword by Mary Jarrell. Appreciation by Robert Lowell. New York: Macmillan, 1985.

Pictures from an Institution: A Comedy. New York: Knopf, 1954.

Poetry and the Age. New York: Knopf, 1953.

Randall Jarrell's Letters: An Autobiographical and Literary Selection. Edited by Mary Jarrell. Boston: Houghton Mifflin, 1985.

A Sad Heart in the Supermarket: Essays and Fables. New York: Atheneum, 1962.

Selected Poems Including "The Woman at the Washington Zoo." New York: Atheneum, 1964.

The Third Book of Criticism. New York: Farrar, Straus and Giroux, 1969.

Translations by Randall Jarrell

Bechstein, Ludwig. *"The Rabbit Catcher" and Other Fairy Tales of Ludwig Bechstein*. Translated with an introduction by Randall Jarrell. Illustrations by Sandro Nardini. New York: Macmillan, 1962.

138

Selected Bibliography

Grimm, Jacob Ludwig Karl and Wilhelm Karl Grimm. *"The Golden Bird" and Other Fairy Tales of the Brothers Grimm*. Translated with an introduction by Randall Jarrell. Illustrated by Sandro Nardini. New York: Macmillan, 1962.

_____. *Snow White and the Seven Dwarfs: A Tale from the Brothers Grimm*. Translated by Randall Jarrell. Pictures by Nancy Ekholm Burkert. New York: Farrar, Straus and Giroux, 1972.

_____. *"The Juniper Tree" and Other Tales by Grimm*. Selected by Maurice Sendak and Lore Segal. Translated by Lore Segal and Randall Jarrell. Pictures by Maurice Sendak. New York: Farrar, Straus and Giroux, 1973.

_____. *The Fisherman and his Wife: A Tale from the Brothers Grimm*. Translated by Randall Jarrell. Pictures by Margot Zemach. New York: Farrar, Straus and Giroux, 1980.

Secondary Sources

Beck, Charlotte H. *Worlds and Lives: The Poetry of Randall Jarrell*. Port Washington, N.Y.: Associated Faculty Press, 1983.

Bettelheim, Bruno. *The Uses of Enchantment: The Meaning and Importance of Fairy Tales*. New York: Knopf, 1976.

Blount, Margaret. *Animal Land: The Creatures of Children's Fiction*. New York: Avon, 1974.

Bryant, J. A., Jr. *Understanding Randall Jarrell*. Columbia: University of South Carolina Press, 1986.

Chesterton, G. K. "The Ethics of Elfland." In *Orthodoxy*. 1909. Reprint. New York: Dodd, Mead, 1957.

Cott, Jonathan. *Pipers at the Gates of Dawn: The Wisdom of Children's Literature*. New York: Random House, 1983.

Dickey, James. "Randall Jarrell." In *RJ, 1914–1965*, 33–48.

Donaghue, Denis. "The Lost World." In *RJ, 1914–1965*, 49–62.

Ferguson, Suzanne. "The Death of Randall Jarrell: A Problem in Legendary Biography." *The Georgia Review* 37 (Winter 1983): 866–76.

———. *The Poetry of Randall Jarrell*. Baton Rouge: Louisiana State University Press, 1971.

Fiedler, Leslie. "Jarrell Criticism: A Footnote." In *RJ, 1914–1965*, 63–69.

Finney, Kathe Davis. "The Poet, Truth, and the Other Fictions: Randall Jarrell as Storyteller." In *Critical Essays*, 284–97.

Getz, Thomas H. "Memory and Desire in *Fly by Night*." *Children's Literature* 11 (1983): 125–34.

Griswold, Jerry. "Fly by Night." *New Republic* 176 (1 January 1977): 30–31. [Review of *Fly by Night*.]

———. "Mother and Child in the Poetry and Children's Books of Randall Jarrell." Ph.D. diss., University of Connecticut, 1980.

Griswold, Jerry, and Edwina Burness. "The Art of Fiction LXXIII: P. L. Travers." *Paris Review* 24 (1982): 208–29.

Hagenbüchle, Helen. *The Black Goddess: A Study of the Archetypal Feminine in the Poetry of Randall Jarrell*. Bern: Francke, 1975.

Hidden, Norman. "'The Moonlit Door': the Child Image in the Poems of Randall Jarrell." *English* 16 (1967): 178–81.

Holtze, Sally Holmes. "A Second Look: *The Animal Family*." *Horn Book Magazine* 61 (November–December 1985): 714–16.

Horn, Bernard. "'The Tongue of Gods and Children': Blakean Innocence in Randall Jarrell's Poetry." *Children's Literature* 2 (1973): 148–51.

Howell, Pamela R. "Voice is Voice Whether a Bat or a Poet: Randall Jarrell's *The Bat-Poet*." In *Proceedings of the Ninth Annual Conference of the Children's Literature Association*, edited by Priscilla A. Ord, 71–76. Iona College, Department of English, 1983.

Jarrell, Mary. "The Animal Family. University of North Carolina—Greensboro *Alumni News* 54 (1966): 24–25.

———. "Ideas and Poems." *Parnassus* 5 (1976): 213–30.

———. Foreword to *The Lost World*, by Randall Jarrell. New York: Macmillan Co., 1985.

———. "The Group of Two." In *RJ, 1914–1965*, 274–98.

———. "Note" to *The Bat-Poet*. Caedmon record TC 1364. New York, 1972.

Kobler, J. F. "Randall Jarrell Seeks Truth in Fantasy." *Forum* 3 (1961): 17–20.

Kunitz, Stanley. "Out of the Cage." In *RJ, 1914–1965,* 97–100.

Lanes, Selma. *The Art of Maurice Sendak.* New York: Abrams, 1980.

Lowell, Robert. "Randall Jarrell." In *RJ, 1914–1965,* 101–12.

Meyers, Jeffrey. "The Death of Randall Jarrell." *Virginia Quarterly Review* 58 (Summer 1982): 450–67.

Moore, Marianne. "Randall Jarrell." In *RJ, 1914–1965,* 125–32.

Neumeyer, Peter F. "Randall Jarrell's *The Animal Family:* New Land and Old." In *Proceedings of the Seventh Annual Conference of the Children's Literature Association,* edited by Priscilla A. Ord, 139–45. Iona College, Department of English, 1982.

———. "Randall Jarrell's *The Bat-Poet:* An Introduction to the Craft." *Children's Literature Association Quarterly* 9 (Summer 1984): 51–53, 59.

Nodelman, Perry. "The Craft or Sullen Art of a Mouse and a Bat." *Language Arts* 55 (April 1978): 467–72, 497.

Quinn, Bernetta, O.S.F. *Randall Jarrell.* Boston: Twayne, 1981.

———. "Warren and Jarrell: The Remembered Child." *Southern Literary Journal* 8 (1976): 24–40.

Rank, Otto. *"The Myth of the Birth of the Hero" and Other Writings.* Edited by Phillip Freund. New York: Alfred A. Knopf, 1932.

Ransom, John Crowe. "The Rugged Way of Genius—A Tribute to Randall Jarrell." In *RJ, 1914–1965,* 155–81.

Rethinger, Alice Marie. "'Slight, Separate, Estranged': The Child and His World in the Poetry of Randall Jarrell." Ph.D. diss., Bowling Green State University, 1975.

Rosenthal, M. L. *Randall Jarrell.* University of Minnesota Pamphlets on American Writers, no. 103. Minneapolis: University of Minnesota Press, 1972.

Sale, Roger. *Fairy Tales and After: From Snow White to E. B. White.* Cambridge: Harvard University Press, 1978.

Sendak, Maurice. "Picture Book Genesis: A Conversation with Maurice Sendak." In *Proceedings of the Fifth Annual Conference of the Children's Literature Association,* edited by Margaret P. Esmonde and Priscilla A. Ord, 29–40. Villanova University, English Department, 1979.

Shapiro, Karl. "The Death of Randall Jarrell." In *RJ 1914–1965*, 195–229.

Travers, P. L. "A Kind of Visitation." In *RJ, 1914–1965*, 253–56.

Updike, John. "Randall Jarrell Writing Stories for Children." In *Critical Essays*, 57–60.

Watson, Robert. "Randall Jarrell: The Last Years." In *RJ, 1914–1965*, 257–73.

Zanderer, Leo. "Randall Jarrell: About and for Children." *The Lion and the Unicorn* 2 (1978): 73–93.

Index

Adoption, 5–6, 37, 48, 51
Andersen, Hans, 100, 127

Bechstein, Ludwig, 2
Blount, Margaret, 40, 42
Burroughs, Edgar Rice. *See*
　Tarzan

Chesterton, G. K., 42
Crane, Hart, 10
Crusoe, Robinson, 96–97, 100

Di Capua, Michael, 1–3, 7–8,
　11–14, 21, 23, 54, 63–64, 103
Dickey, James, xiv

Fathers, 119–20
Ferguson, Suzanne, 117
Fiedler, Leslie, xi

Freud, Sigmund, 20, 89, 93,
　121, 122
Frost, Robert, xi, 10, 52, 54–58

"The Gingerbread Boy," 23–24
Grimm, 2–3, 21, 23, 25, 42, 76,
　82, 85. *See also individual tales*

"Hansel and Gretel," 30, 35–37,
　45, 82, 93, 119, 121, 129–30
Hawthorne, Nathaniel, 54, 134
　(n. 5)

"Jack and the Beanstalk," 32
Jarrell, Mary, 11, 53, 54–56, 59,
　65, 96–98
Jarrell, Randall
　BOOKS OF POETRY: *Blood for a*
　Stranger, 129; *Little Friend*,
　Little Friend, 97, 129; *Losses*,